A Lifetime Fight- Living with Cerebral Palsy

Amanda Forry/Fino

Published by Independently published, 2023.

While every precaution has been taken in the preparation of this book, the publisher assumes no responsibility for errors or omissions, or for damages resulting from the use of the information contained herein.

A LIFETIME FIGHT- LIVING WITH CEREBRAL PALSY

First edition. March 1, 2023.

ISBN: 979-8215869000

Written by Amanda Forry/Fino.

PREFACE

I am looking back today with a better of my past! I truly ponder; Was it me, My mother, who could not accept my condition, the children I wanted to be accepted by, my inability to perform nor keep up with the schooling agenda, wanting to be accepted? Frustration with my having cerebral palsy and knowing this disorder will be with me for the rest of my life. I cannot put my finger on any one thing. Most likely all. I do know; it has been a hard road. So hurtful at times that I wanted to end it all. However, I have found a path to keep me strong, believe in others, and feel for those less fortunate. My belief in religion and its heavenly blanket makes it much more comfortable for me and gives me the drive to understand and acceptance for my condition.

Do not get me wrong; it is hard and blocks my future of many of my desires. I am a woman with the sexual desires that come with it, knowing they may never be fulfilled.

My writings below point out how I felt at those times. I do not feel that way today. Back then, I blamed others without pointing the finger at myself. I have changed! I still have temper tantrums, but now they are more controllable. The church, my new parents, my Godmother, and my friends have been a beacon of hope for me. I forgive all those who hurt me and my feelings, and I can only pray that they forgive me. I genuinely thank all of you who have come to know me.

I dedicate this written journey to all of you.

PROLOGUE

Flying on an airplane has always scared me since I'm afraid of heights, and I had been on one before 9/11. Since then, I have refused to fly on a plane. Except once. My mom made me fly on one when we went to Charleston, South Carolina, from Las Vegas, Nevada, for Thanksgiving 2012, a trip that I sometimes forget since it was very fast and short.

When we got on that airplane, I fell in love with flying. I was treated like a V.I.P. with my disability, having someone who knew their way around the vast airport and pushed me around in a wheelchair.

While living in Pahrump, Nevada, in April 2016, I was homeless after my mother left me at a counseling center in the middle of the session after making no sense and walking out, shutting the door. The image is still in my mind. When I did not find her in the waiting room, I called her, and she told me she wouldn't come to pick me up. If I came back home, she would call the cops, she said. I only wanted to talk to my counselor about our latest mother-daughter fights.

By now, I had become afraid of her, my birth mother. Then it hit me with a numb feeling—I was homeless. I had to think fast of someone I know to call Ronald Fino, a father-like figure I met a while back. Since then, we have been in touch via Facebook, yet I didn't have my phone or anything.

They let me use the office computer to log into my Facebook account first, hoping to keep my password manageable since I was shaking like never before. I hoped that Ronald was on, seeing the green light on his picture.

I quickly typed him, what is your number? I need to call you now. He replied right back. I called him as soon as possible, and we talked with the aid of another person who understood my speech impairment. Ron offered to have me fly back east to Williamsburg, VA, where he and his family live.

I was lucky that Britney, my little sister, showed up at the counseling center with my laptop and phone. Someone asked her why she wasn't taking me home, and she was like, take her. Or was it me, remembering that Britney shot me a nasty look when our eyes met? My eyes were full of hate, now looking back at her.

In the meantime, the counseling center contacted the women's shelter and took me there. I was so lost. A women's shelter—wow, I never imagined that I would be at a women's shelter. When I got there, "Joni," my new caseworker at this women's shelter, told me they would pay for my ticket if Ronald and his wife agreed. We were all on the same page, yet it was too late in the day to make plans to fly out.

They took me to a hidden women's shelter. I had nothing on me except the clothes I was wearing, a laptop, a cell phone, and my medication. By now, I felt like I was homeless. Joni showed me a room and tried to get something for me. A woman there took me under her wing and helped me out. I was continually thankful for her.

At last, alone in this room, I let myself feel and let my hurting feelings out—26 years of bottled-up crying. I did not expect my mother to do this to me, and I knew that I had lost my family. My "Gagwa" finally called me back when she returned from being in Las Vegas (her home in Pahrump, Nevada, was 45 miles from Las Vegas).

My "grandma" was shocked and upset to learn about my day. She wanted to know where I was, but I couldn't tell her because I couldn't tell her, and besides, I didn't know where this home was. I just gave her Joni's cell phone number so my "grandma" could call.

The day after the next, I found myself at the airport in Las Vegas, ready to fly on my own. I was terrified because it was something I had never done. Also, this was one of the worst times in my life. I prayed to God to help me on that day. Joni's help getting me on the plane was a blessing. I bid her goodbye, leaving her at the gate.

I was very emotional, but I was seated by this man who "talked" to me through my laptop. We had a friendly conversation as I told him a part of my story. I told everyone that I was seeing my "Uncle Ron." I figured it would be safer and easier to say, "I'm going to see my uncle." Since I have a speech impairment, I've found that laptops and Smartphones are the best way to connect with people.

I had a short layover, and I called my grandmother, and she told me that she had just seen my mom and sister and heard that I had left the state. I forgot all that was said and spoken, but it didn't sound good.

I got on my next airplane to Washington, DC. I will never forget flying over D.C. at night with a sigh of relief—I made it out. Here I am in the U.S. Capitol. God had a hand in this as I saw Ronald smiling right out the main door with his white MR2. We drove from D.C. to his house. Now six years later, I can recall that day flying home at last!

I am here, still "flying" today as a self-advocate. A proud Virginian and a concerned citizen. A member of the Training Alumni Association (T.A.A.)—an association of the Partners in Policymaking program graduates and the Youth Leadership Academy supported by the Virginia Board for People with Disabilities that facilitates grassroots advocacy. I am a proud graduate of the class of 2020.

I was born with cerebral palsy because of a difficult birth. However, I have decided to wear my cerebral palsy as a "badge of courage." My cerebral palsy is what is called Mixed Type cerebral palsy. I have muscle spasms, making it hard to relax. I have no control over my voice tones, and these two are the parts I hate. I cannot work a real job.

I believe that I have a grammatical learning disability as one of my quirks. We all have them, and some people have problems remembering names! My problems include grammar and spelling issues, which my mind doesn't recognize. PTSD can also accompany cerebral palsy.

When most people think of PTSD, they think of soldiers on the battlefield. Sadly, however, post-traumatic stress can affect anyone who has survived traumatic events regardless of background. My formative years were difficult because of a dysfunctional family experience that spanned three states and took me out of mainstream education.

I was isolated in my youth by homeschooling and not receiving the needed treatments like O.T., P.T., Speech Therapy, and pediatric visits. I have endured many traumatic childhood experiences, including physical, mental, sexual, and emotional abuse that led to my PTSD and Bipolar disorder.

While coping with my father's death from cancer at age fifty-nine, my biological mother changed from a loving mother to someone who struggled to love me, which resulted in her having me locked up through my teen years in my own family home.

My mom led me to believe that anger and hate were the way to live. I've survived three murder attempts by her hand. I felt like an animal, a monster that needed to be locked up. My mom tried to get me locked up in a mental asylum or a group home for disabled people so she could forget about me. She acted like I was never her daughter on several occasions, near the near edge of life, until I opened the Bible to read God's word and meet my savior Jesus Christ.

During our conversations, I discussed my desire to find a good neighborhood church with my recently connected Godmother, Liz. Also, I've talked about finding a church with Dad for a while.

Using Google to search "church near me," I discovered a Presbyterian (P.C.A.) Church with values similar to mine that seemed like they fit. Note: my Godmother's pastor texted her back that moment, saying it was the only church he would have recommended in Williamsburg! Lucky me, it was only some of the way across town.

On August 8, My new dad "Ron Fino" and I visited this Presbyterian Church after introducing myself via email and explaining myself and my cerebral palsy. Moments after stepping into its open window chapel, I knew I had found what I was looking for in my lifetime, welcome home Amanda. As if this was waiting for me to find, I was at peace and peace with God. It was a place I could see myself growing in, growing older, and taking this church as my second home.

Within a few weeks, I seemed to like this church more. I met my beloved sister and Bible teacher Cyndi, her husband, and her mom.

As a result, I joined their six-week discovery course. I just had to decide whether or not this church was the right one for me. I joined the church, upholding my vows and showing my commitment. Getting baptized at my new church was especially important since I was never baptized as a child.

During my baptism in November, everyone watching was moved as if the Holy Spirit came upon us and gave me a new heart. As stated in the Bible, I will give you a new heart and put a new spirit within you; I will take the heart of stone out of your flesh and give you a heart of flesh. (Ezekiel 36:26 NKJV) God indeed put into me a new heart along with a new set of eyes like Paul on the road to Damascus.

That was one of the most important days of my life. Since then, I have fully embraced being part of my church while making new friends. The Christmas eve church candlelight service is delightful to me. The Women's Ministry at my church enables me to grow in the grace and truth to become a better woman. I have seen hope and joy in myself that can only come from God. He continues to have lots of work within me through the Spirit to overcome anger, fear, shame, and doubt when they arise.

I desire to share my story of coming to faith with other disabled people, talking about God's love, helping them with their disabilities, preparing videos on my YouTube Chanel, Cerebral Palsy Gal's World, and speaking on the internet. My vision is to make the church more inclusive to those with disabilities. My goal is to educate others on how to welcome them and make church a more enjoyable experience rather than making them feel judged for their disability or the life choices they are forced to make because of it.

In the interest of full disclosure, this is my autobiography written before I turned to Jesus and became a Christian. When deciding whether or not I preferred to rewrite the work or leave it as it was, I had to make a great deal of effort deciding. As a result, many hours of prayer and meditation were dedicated to this project. However, on the other hand, the Lord has led me to overcome and compelled me to share my experience with you. There is no doubt that Christians have faced hardship at some point in their lives, and surprisingly, I don't have to be embarrassed about my past any longer as I grow in faith.

I am sure that not everyone will be able to read my book; for example, some will be crying too much and therefore not be able to read - some may disagree with what I did in my past. Despite that, that is okay because it encourages us as Christians to grow in our relationship with God.

Las Vegas, 1990

During lunch at their desks, Liz and Linda talked about Linda and her husband, Matt Forrie, for nine years. They attempted to conceive using an ordinary method, gave up hope of having a child, and used their savings to build a pool. She complained that she was feeling queasy and wasn't sure why.

Liz asked Linda when was the last period she had, and Linda was prompted to believe that it was a late period. During lunch, the two of them rushed to a nearby drugstore. Liz had purchased Linda a Clearblue Easy Pregnancy Test, thinking Linda might be pregnant, but Linda was disbelieving. When Linda realized she was pregnant, she used the pharmacy bathroom to check.

A pregnancy test was conducted for three minutes before Linda could believe she was expecting a child. Linda was unable to believe what they were seeing. However, they purchased all types of pregnancy tests to ensure that Lind was expecting a child. Having gotten positive results on all tests, Linda named Liz the Godmother of her newborn baby. This baby that was growing inside Linda was me.

My due date was April 1, 1990, but I didn't deliver. A cesarean section was scheduled for April 7, 1990, at 8 am, and my birth doctor was taking her sweet time, making me wait.

My umbilical cord wrapped around my neck, cutting off the air circulation to my head at 1:14 pm, was the moment that I, Amanda Victoria Forrie, entered the world - blue.

As a child, I remember this story, my Godfather from my dad's side, Bruno, figuring out how to flip me over to make me look like a pancake in the sunlight, so I could develop color on my body by bringing me to the sunny window to "bake."

The doctors weren't doing a great job with me, so Bruno didn't care what they thought. Although I don't recall why Bruno was able to bring more color to me by getting rid of the blue, I am eternally grateful for his help. I would lay in the sun wave also improves my cerebral palsy.

My family and close friends gathered to celebrate my birth since my parents had been trying to conceive for ten years. I was brought home by limo by my parents. A year later, my mom took another pregnancy test, and the result was blue. My dad said, "That's a bit blue." She replied, "I guess that's a bit pregnant." Fifteen months later, Britney, my little sister, was born on July 21, 1991

As a child, my family noticed that I held the bottle incorrectly. It took a long time for my parents to figure out the problem, taking me to several doctors to do the same. As a child, someone told my parents I would never talk, walk, or be an empty shell, so they should put me in a home. The physical therapist finally told them I had cerebral palsy. As you can see, I have proved that person wrong.

By then, my mother had given up her job at the Las Vegas metro police station to raise Britney and me. In the kitchen one day, my mom tried to get me to say mommy, but my dad walked in, and I saw him and said, "Daddy."

My early memories are of Britney taking me by the hand and teaching me to walk in our home hallway, and I used a walker and got around on my knees. My entire family was amazed when I stood up one day and ran down a hill to join in the fun of playing with my sister and cousins.

I remember being on my grandparents' boat on Lake Mean, going to my dad's company picnics, parties, and holidays, and even going to Disneyland twice. I am telling you, the Forrie family was a party-throwing family! Life was enjoyable in those days. I remember my dad's big brother, uncle Kenny and my grandma Margaret Forrie, who was always at our house. I loved her very much. My dad came from a huge family with three sisters: Tammy, Naomi, and Linda, all the same name as my mom.

Even though my Grandpa Forrie was still living in 2022, he has been obsolete in my life since birth for reasons I cannot explain. I only knew him twice, and neither experience was pleasant. As a token of respect, I would like to acknowledge my two twin uncles, Uncle John, and Uncle James Forrie. Both of them died at birth, about a year after my dad.

During my childhood, I spent every Saturday with my grandparents, Joseph and Betty Anderson, who were my mom's parents. Since I find it challenging to say grandma, I called Betty my "grandma," and Joseph was my "Papa." Britney and I grew up playing with our cousins James and Alyssa at Gragwa's house, and they became like my older brother and sister than cousins.

My grandparents' first-born son, James, was the only son of Uncle David and Aunt Shelby. Alyssa was only daughter. Uncle Chuck and Aunt Lilly, my mother's other bother. My mother were my grandparents' last born. Playing around my Grragwa's and Papa's house was one of my fondest memories.

I grew up with my grandma, and over time, we grew fond of each other, forming a special bond of love and friendship that continues to this day. I always looked up to my grandma, and I still do. I can't express how much I love and value her.

My first friend was Tiffany Parker. We were the same age, and my dad and mom were friends with her parents, Peter and Kelly Parker. The Parkers met my parent through work and became good buddies, along with Linda and Kelly, both pregnant at the same time. Tiffany and I played together as children. Tiffany also had a sister, Nicole, who was younger, and we would go off and leave Britney and Nicole to play, and Britney didn't like it.

I loved watching Barney, America's favorite purple dinosaur, as a kid. I watched PBS kids' shows, Nickelodeon, Disney, and movies. My passion for Broadway shows and movies began at an early age as my mother played all of Rodgers and Hammerstein's movies on Britney and me. I would always be inside and fall asleep watching Mary Poppins. As a movie buff, I also watched the latest films when my mom let me.

My dad would get dressed for work early in the morning, and I would wait quietly in the doorway of his room with my bottle in hand. After I gave my father my bottle, he filled it up. When he returned my bottle to me, I went back to bed. It was a routine that I followed every day.

I remember going to speech, physical, and occupational therapy in my childhood, and I had the pleasure of seeing a variety of people with disabilities, some of whom were more severe than my own. Once, a full-grown head was seen on a baby's body. I also had the opportunity to attend a particular swimming class at a pool in Las Vegas. I am a big fan of water; swimming is an integral part of my life. My home had a swimming pool, where Britney and I took private lessons in our pool. When I was three, my parents put me in a particular education school where I learned to write, sing, play dress-up, and learn. I was in school plays where we would sing and act. When Britney yelled out loud and interrupted my school's Christmas play, my grandmother stopped her with her finger over her mouth. It wasn't very comfortable for me. I was once in a commercial.

I remember my father working for Tommy Jensen, a car dealership owner who took an interest in me and my cerebral palsy. After Tommy asked my parents if we could make a T.V. commercial together, my parents agreed. I remember sitting on Tom's lap and feeling like a star in the commercial. As a result, I received unique items that helped me with my cerebral palsy.

Two teachers from my school came to my house one day, taking many pictures of me at home. I can't remember why, but I had fun. I was even making a school movie. I always dreamed of becoming an actor if I did not have cerebral palsy. I enjoyed school. My only problem was that I was smarter than my classmates and friends.

At six, I started my primary education at the Altman Elementary School. My parents chose to place me in a mainstream school. There I was, a six-year-old going to first grade. My new school was my favorite. I had Mr. Aksum as my teacher. I had Mrs. Blue as my Special Education teacher and Mrs. Callan as my Special Education teacher. I had a full-time aide named Martha, who was very kind to me. I became fast friends with a girl named Lindsey.

Meanwhile, my parents decided they didn't want me and Britney to grow up in Las Vegas, so they found a small town in Utah called Delta instead. We sold our home; after that, my dad left us to find a job at its small car dealership. I was not happy with him being away. I used to sleep with my mom at night because I feared being away from him. The weekends were always a good time when my dad came home.

I didn't want to move to Delta and leave my beloved grandma, family, and friends, so my parents allowed me to finish 1st grade in Las Vegas. My mom initially drove Britney and me up to see my father in Delta, and he lived in a motel for some reason I didn't understand. It was great to see him, and we watched The Three Stooges. Most of the time, I did not go to see him, so I stayed with my grandma and Papa and went to school instead.

The one time my dad took me to a hockey game, it was a school event during which all my friends, classmates, and teachers were present to celebrate the home team's win. It was a blast; we were all rooting for the home team to win.

One day I had a crush on a boy in a wheelchair, and we were working on something, and we got it right. I was so happy that I kissed him. Boy, my mother wasn't pleased when I told her about my first kiss. I remember either I lost a tooth while kissing him or he did – I can't remember from the back of my head if I lost a tooth while kissing him or not.

The summer of 1997 was one of the worst times for me because I had to say goodbye to all my loved ones at Altman Elementary. My childhood home became a loved memory, having no choice but to leave for Delta, Utah.

Delta, Utah 1997

During the 4th of July parade in our 'new' town, Britney and I rode in a covered wagon with his granddaughter, who was also Britney's age. My dad's friend owned a covered wagon. We threw candy at the other kids, then watched the fireworks at his house.

As part of our relocation to Delta, we took Bo, who was boarded at Pat and Lisa King's horse ranch. The apartment we found was tiny, with just two bedrooms, and Britney and I shared a room and slept on an airbed until we got bunk beds. We moved up to Delta with the help of Alyssa and her father, Uncle Chuck, my mother's older brother.

I remember waking up to a dear handmade card by Alyssa on the first day of 2nd grade at Delta North Elementary School, the home of the Busy Bees at that time. Mrs. Frandsen and her husband placed me in a class with the best classroom teacher in 2nd grade, Carol Frandsen. She was terrific, and she took care of my whole family well. I will never forget her and her husband.

The school's principal was Mr. Noah, and the special education teacher was Mrs. Hanson, who helped me with my occupational and physical therapy. Since the town was so small, there was no such facility. I met new friends during my class and realized that moving was okay.

Life in Delta was all right. School events and hanging out at the horse ranch kept me busy. I learned to ride a horse bareback. Was it scary to ride an animal so big? The horse would walk while someone held my hand. Over time, I did not need any special equipment. The fact is that horseback riding offers the perfect therapy for people with cerebral palsy and disabilities. I discovered Pat Parelli's Horsemanship in 2006 and met Pat Parelli at a two-day event. At one point, I was able to lay on a horse bareback.

My parents had then bought a small white house off the main street. It had three bedrooms and one bathroom, and I loved that backyard.

As part of our move into our new town, my mother took Britney and me to the Mormon Church. Though I am now a Presbyterian, I remember saying my prayers every night and understanding hell and heaven. I am unsure about the Bible because my mother told me it contains numerous lies about men. Since I became a church member today, I have realized that the Bible is God's word and that Jesus is my savior. Grandma's teachings taught me that God is everywhere, including trees, water, lakes, flowers, grass, etc.

As a result, we discovered that family members lived in Delta by marriage, so we used to get together occasionally. Britney and I occasionally visited a babysitter at her house. Her name was Cammy, and she had two daughters my age and a boy. We had an exciting time. Through the horse ranch, my mom became friends with Jenny and Tim. They live next door to Pat and Terri King's horse ranch and have their horses. Horses were a huge part of our Delta life. Britney and I soon bought Rock and sold Bo since Rock was kinder to ride.

Also, I was a cheerleader for Britney's soccer team, and Mrs. Frandsen made me my outfit. I wish that I still had it.

When I was fooling around with friends at school, I fell, splitting my head open. They rushed me to the hospital. It was not my first time busting my head. I once fell in my Gragwa's hallway knocking my head, but never like this. I remember laughing so hard that I fell. I remember screaming out while the doctor stitched my head back together and having to tie me down on the table. I don't remember how old I was at the time.

Papa and grandma saw us often, or we went to Las Vegas to see them and their family. We stayed in a log cabin on a fishing trip, telling ghost stories until late at night. It was a family affair, and my father liked fishing. The fishing was too dull, so I dropped my pole and wandered off to play. The funny thing was I always caught fish. Ha!

During my school years, there were a lot of aids available to me, but one of them was mean to me. One day, I was so hurt that I blocked it out of my mind, so I could not honestly explain what had happened. It only occurred to me that my mom saw the whole thing, and the woman never worked with me again. All my classmates, including Mrs. Frandsen and Mrs. Hanson, attended during my eighth birthday party at McDonald's.

There was once a time when I was terrible at Britney's soccer practice. The boy I liked picked on another boy, knocking him to the ground and putting grass on his underwear. My mom saw what I did and punished me. I also remember one night fighting with my parents, and I packed my bag and tried to run away, but I couldn't bring myself to open the front door. We all made up, however.

I had a unique desk at school that made doing my schoolwork easier. I had difficulty learning to read, understand money, tell time, and learn math, but science was never a problem. Art and history were my favorite subjects. I also remember spending a happy time in Mrs. Hanson's classroom. It was my favorite aid at the time - I can't remember her name - who gave me a book about a man with a disability who found true love in awe and was captivated by that book.

Mrs. Frandsen always took my mom, Britney, and me all over the town to events or church events. Once, we went to a horse fair with Pat up by Salt Lake. I remember it was pitch black and snowing, and it was tricky to drive through the snow at four or five am.

Mrs. Frandsen introduced us to an old lady in the church. She wanted to be Britney's and my God-Grandmother. I felt unfaithful to grandma, so I presented Grandma with a card instead. I never played with Britney much, but she once gave me a black eye and a bloody nose for fighting on her bed. I even played with my Barbies and dressed up alone. Britney sometimes played along with me, but I usually played alone most of the time. I fell in love with American Girl, but I never had an American Girl doll, and I always loved looking at them in magazines. To this day, I still want an American Girl doll.

A rumor began at my dad's workplace in the spring or summer of 1998. Since we weren't Mormons and we didn't fit in, despite our best efforts, they wanted a Mormon working for them. Then my dad got a new job, and we plan moving up to Portland, Oregon. I was sad because we were so far from my grandma.

Maria, my mother's best friend, came to town with her two children, Tara and Ryan, one weekend. We showed them the best of Delta and went home to have a B.B.Q. and watch Home Alone 3.

The summer school was fun, and Mrs. Frandsen taught my class. I had a blast learning '50s songs and performing a '50s play for our parents. My Papa and grandma came up to watch Britney and me for a week. My parents went up to Portland to find a house to rent. Also, to have some romantic time by the sea. What a great week; it still makes me smile to reflect on it.

As the big move to Portland, Oregon, approached, my dad and I rode to pick up the U-Haul in a town that was two hours away. Everyone helped us pack up the house quickly. Britney and I went for one last game with our friends. Saying goodbye to everyone was hard.

Portland, Oregon

Moving has been a nightmare! The U-Haul broke down in the middle of nowhere, my cat vomited and peed in its carrier, and I peed on the hotel bedding. After three days, we arrived in Portland. On the first night of our trip, we stayed at a pleasant hotel with a sandbox and a swimming pool.

In Boring, Oregon, a suburb of Portland. The home was located on the borderline between Happy Valley and Boring, and we lived in Happy Valley and attended school there.

A two-sided river rock fireplace, a large home movie theater, and a sunroom made the house one of the most incredible places to live. It had three bedrooms, two bathrooms, and a large home movie theater. Although it was my favorite house by far, we only rented it. I had a bigger room because I was older. Britney had a tiny room with a vast built-in desk that fit her bed.

It was fun to see Portland with my grandma and Papa. I had never seen a city like Portland before. Portland was full of history, art, and culture. The very well-to-do lived in Happy Valley, so there were tons of huge mansions in the area, and it was great for Halloween candy.

I attended Happy Valley Elementary School as a student. Mr. Kleiner told my mom he would be the principal for as long as I was there. I was placed in Mrs. Weston's third-grade classroom, and Erin was my full-time aide. On the playground, I hung out with Kristen, Laura, Sydney, Natalie, Kaylee, Kayla, Amy, and many other girls I met. During third grade, a girl named Jessica was kind to me, but it wasn't until fourth grade that we became soul sisters.

I enjoyed the third grade. In the third grade, I discovered my hero, Helen Keller, about whom I wrote a report, but was penalized because Mr. Weston believed my mother did the work, not me. As a result of this, I disliked Mr. Weston. Happy Valley Elementary was extremely strict on the school work. I always had much homework to do the next day, and I did my homework before dinner and was done by then.

The school was great. We had the best school field trips that I loved going on. We saw the Portland Symphony Orchestra, the art museum, plays, etc. I used to play at Kristen's or Laura's house. As a Christmas gift, Erin took me, Kristen, and Laura to see The Rugrats Movie. I sat next to Bethany, and we were kind to each other. One day, she turned Kristen and Laura away from me. It made me wonder what I did to make her turn against me.

During my time at Portland Shriners Hospital, I was treated in several ways that benefited me. They provided me with my first laptop computer, which inspired me to write. My laptop was old and, unfortunately, disappeared. What happened to my laptop; I don't know where it went. My dearest dreams of becoming a published author have come true because of Portland Shriners Hospital.

As I woke up sad, my mother asked me if anything was wrong at school. I replied, "Are there any other cerebral palsy patients who aren't lifeless or wheelchair confined?".

As a result, my mom got in touch with someone, and I met this older sixteen-year-old girl with crutches. We used to talk at her work, In and Out Burger, and she had cerebral palsy, but I can't seem to remember too much about her.

My parents bought our biggest house, a two-story home with three bedrooms and three bathrooms. We tried to buy it, but the property owner wouldn't sell it. The property owner wasn't kind to us and didn't want kids in her house. So, we found this house and moved in.

For my ninth birthday, my grandma and Papa came up. My father went fishing with my Papa, and my mother and grandma planned a big birthday party. My party theme was Rugrats because I loved it. We played games, danced, and played around. I got beautiful gifts too. I had an exciting time!

After my dad started drinking after work, I rarely saw him, and I wasn't able to understand my parents' endless fighting and my dad's drinking. Suddenly, my mom drove away after a big fight, and I wasn't sure if she'd come home that day. However, she returned three hours later.

My sister and I wore Goodwill clothes and ate the same food every day at our school. When my mother was angry, she would turn up the radio in her car to the maximum. She talked with the women at Albertson's grocery store for hours. The other half of the time, I lived in my imagination. That summer of 1999, Britney turned eight, and we went to the beach with grandma and Papa and enjoyed the seaside.

It was not all sunshine that summer. One morning, my mom beat me by washing my hair and nearly killed me in the bathwater. She was mad at me, and I wasn't sure why. It turns out that I used the last bath salt I had. I apologized and did not say anything. When she told me to wash the shampoo out of my hair, she held me underwater with her hands pushing downward, drowning me. At the time, I was too scared and young to realize what was happening. It was a good thing she stopped and acted as if nothing had happened.

My mother admitted that she was the worst mother, never apologizing. She made me promise not to tell anyone, including my father, and I pushed it far down in my mind to forget it.

My dad and Aunt Naomi would have loved for me to have told them that night, but I regret not doing so now.

The time Aunt Naomi flew in for a beautiful week was filled with many fun activities. A few days later, her new husband, my new Uncle Tony, arrived and left for their honeymoon. While playing with Britney later, Luis Logan, the Girl Scout leader, called me and asked me if I was interested in being a girl scout in his troop.

Girl Scout

I remember driving up to Luis Logan's mansion and being impressed by his mansion. Luis Logan was the father of Amy, a tycoon. Luis hosted an end-of-summer party at his house. Luis and Kelly welcomed the new girl scouts to the troop party. Luis and Kelly were very kind to my Mom, Britney, and me.

Upon entering the large playroom, we found the other girls I knew from school: Amy, Sydney, Natalie, Kaylee, Kayla, Melissa, Claire, Rachel, Mckayla, and I. There were ten of us, and Mckayla and I were the newest girl scouts. We spent the afternoon swimming in Logan's pool, playing around the house, and talking. Luis showed us how to make honey, and we all got a jar to take home.

Because Britney was also a girl scout in another troop, my parents took Britney and me to the girl scout store on Saturday to purchase our uniforms and workbooks. After the ladies asked what troop I was in, they were amazed and told my parents that it was like Troop Beverly Hills, the 1989 movie come to life.

My teacher was Mrs. Hudson when I began 4th grade, and I discovered that my desk was next to Jessica's. I enjoyed learning about Oregon Trail history during my 4th grade year, and I had a crush on a boy named Jack ever since I saw him for the first time. When I played alone with Jack during recess, it was almost as if we were going out on a date.

A girl scout in 4th grade was like a cheerleader in high school. One girl was jealous of me because I was one, but she wasn't. Sydney quit the troop after something upset her. We rented a radio station from Luis once, and once, he rented out a Delta Airlines plane so we could experience first-class seats and a view of the cockpit of an airplane. For us to learn about fresh flowers from Hawaii, Luis flew them into our classroom. Additionally, we went to clown school, which I found utterly unbelievable.

It was a great self-esteem boost for me back then, being the only disabled kid at school, hanging out, and being best buddies with rich kids. I was a lucky duck. It was annoying that my Mom had to attend every girl scout event since all the other girls' moms were absent. In those days, my mother was seen by others as a supermom, and it went unnoticed that she was not that way when others were not present.

Our family went to the beach one day when we were off work and school. We saw The Prince of Egypt in our hotel room, jumped in the pool, and played on the swing set together, and I will never forget my dad's remark: "A family that swims together stays together." We enjoyed riding the town's merry-go-round and a four-seater bike, and everyone had a wonderful time.

As my friendship grew, I spent more time with Jessica, and we talked for hours. The Christmas of 1999 was a busy time. My dad took us all to his company's big Christmas party. We had a Christmas party at school, and my grandparents flew to be with us. We had a great time, and Santa gave me a gift.

As Y2K approached, I didn't understand the significance. I spent the new millennium playing with Jessica at home and attending a party at my dad's coworker's house. No harm came to the world that night - a peaceful day at my home on January 1, 2000. For two weeks, the whole 4th-grade class took swimming lessons at Girls, those excellent indoor pools, somewhere in Clackamas county, Oregon.

Britney, Jessica, and Megan went to Chuck E. Cheese on my tenth birthday and had a great time. My parents gave me my first CD player and three C.D.s, which began my love of music.

While Britney was in her acting class, my parents and I hung out in downtown Portland every Saturday while Britney attended her class. Living in Portland was a wonderful experience for me.

My family always attended Portland Shriners Hospital events. The Portland Shriners helped me, teaching me new ways to simplify life. By now, I could talk, walk, and write independently. My Mom always cut up my food, and I always used a drinking straw. Although I was a good student, I could not read a book to save my life.

Jack stopped hanging out at school and wouldn't talk to me. Later, through the grapevine, I discovered that Sydney was telling Jack bad things about me, which is why he wasn't interested in me. Sydney was a friend of mine, and we played with her Barbie collection at her big blue house. I thought she liked Jack too, which is why she did it. Although devastated, I kept it inside since I was busy with other friends.

We soon were getting ready for our significant girl scout troop trip to Silver Falls, Oregon. We sold cookies to raise money for our cookie sale. We had hoped to fly to Hawaii, but Luis refused, so we headed camping instead. Understandably my Mom wouldn't let me go alone, like always, so I had to wait for my dad, and we all went to the camp on Saturday morning. While I had been hoping to go camping with my friends on Friday morning without my entire family, I made the most of it.

I had a blast! Amy, Kayla, Rachel, and I had a blast in my tent. After horseback riding and hiking, we spent much time playing and sitting around the campfire, and I know what it means to have fun. During the night, we stayed up telling ghost stories in our tent until we got yelled at, so we went to bed.

The next morning was Father's Day. My Mom had to pull me away from my friends to go into our family tent to wish my dad a happy Father's Day. Amy had written a funny Father's Day song for Dad. The song made me laugh hard, but someone didn't like it, so we had to develop a better song. Then we had to pack up camp, but everyone had a great time.

I liked Tiffany. She lived two houses down from ours, and she and Britney took me to the zoo for her summer birthday. I went to Jessica's house for Jessica's tenth birthday after Britney and I had a pool party. My first sleepover.

Later, my Papa called to tell us that he and g were moving to a small town near Las Vegas called Pahrump, Nevada. I was sad since I used to spend every Saturday at their house, and I loved the house where my Mom was raised.

During summer school, I also discovered my love of storytelling and writing. I wrote a short story about a girl who solved a mystery in London. She loved the story so much that she hung it behind her desk. She said I should consider becoming an author someday. At the time, I was planning to become a teacher, and I still wonder if she has my story behind her desk to this day.

In 5th grade, he decided not to be a troop leader anymore. That was a sad day for me. My fifth-grade year could have been more pleasant. Despite a new school opening and a shift in the school district, Jessica and my friends were no longer in my class. Happy Valley now had a classroom for troubled kids.

In my home, things were going poorly. My Mom, my sister Britney, and I started our girl scout troop. My dad's friend and an old coworker offered him a job in Escondido, California, one day. It's a small world, as my Mom was born there. I grew up in Oceanside, California, and my g grew up there.

My Mom made him take the job because she disliked all the rain in Portland. Once, it rained non-stop for three weeks. Portland receives substantial rainfall. Eventually, the rain started affecting my Mom, and I'm sorry to say that's when her depression began. When I heard the news, I was distraught. It was yet another move I would have to make, and it was not something I wanted to happen.

On the Internet, my Mom found a two-bedroom apartment that had just opened. I had Jessica over for one last sleepover. We would have family nearby, which was good. g and Papa were nearer, so we could see them more. It was a sad night, but my Mom made it fun. My dad had already gone to California to start his new job. So my grandma helped my Mom pack up the house.

One day after school, I found my room packed with boxes and vomited on them. My Mom made me stay home from school the following day, but I didn't want to because that day, I would hear the Portland Symphony Orchestra on my school field trip with my grandma. I had always wanted to take my grandma to the Portland Symphony Orchestra.

As it rained, it was challenging to say goodbye to all my good friends, Jessica, and great friends. After school, we got into the car and left for good. All the fun times we had in Portland and all the family day trips were no more. I cried like a baby. Since that sad day, I have never returned.

Escondido, California

Grandma and my Mom fought the whole way to Escondido. I felt sad because my cat was ill. We had two cars: my Mom drove with her two cats, grandma with Britney, and I with her cat. We could not use cell phones, so we kept in touch via walkie-talkies. In three days and two nights, we arrived in Escondido.

We arrived in Escondido to find our beds set up by my dad and the mover. The apartment was a nice place to live. After dinner and going to bed, we went to see what Escondido had to offer the next day when my dad was off work. We visited the Oceanside harbor and ate fish and chips. I will never forget an old woman on her bicycle who looked like the Wicked Witch of the West. My dad sang the wicked witch theme song, and it was funny.

When grandma returned home, it was time to enroll in school. Rock Springs Elementary School was close by. Two ladies from the school district came to our apartment to talk to my Mom and me about going to another school across town. We visited that school, and my Mom and I decided that Rock Springs would better fit me.

As it was a year-round school, Britney and I had to start school back up in January. During the holidays, we visited my grandma's family. We were at Uncle Peter's house on Thanksgiving and had lunch with Sue. Great Aunt Audrey's husband, Uncle Pet, and her only sister, Gagwa, gave birth to two sons, Uncle Kevin, and Uncle Ray. When I was young, she died of the Big C.

My uncle Ray, Aunt Pam, and their kids, Alexis and Ellie, were at Thanksgiving dinner with me. Uncle Kevin and his son Ryan lived in Las Vegas when I was a child, and he was close in age to my parents. We had a wonderful Thanksgiving dinner, with beautiful weather. Sue took a family photo of me, Mom, Britney, and myself. Then Uncle Pet placed a red rose on Aunt Audrey's grave after dinner. Even though I was only ten, it was evident that Uncle Pet still loved her very much.

My parents asked Uncle Ray and Aunt Pam if Alexis, sixteen, could babysit Britney and me for a night. They agreed, so my Mom dropped us off at their house. Alexis, Ellie, Britney, and I were left alone because Uncle Ray and Aunt Pam went out somewhere. We all had a wild time swimming in the outdoor spa, splashing in the big tub, laughing, and having fun. The time was 1 am when I crawled into bed, the longest I had ever stayed up. My great Aunt Audrey smiled down on us from Heaven as we had a ball.

My Mom took Britney and me to visit my grandparents in Pahrump, NV, for a week. I thought Pahrump was trashy, with old mobile homes around, when I first visited it. Then we drove into the more attractive part of Pahrump, where my grandparents had built their new house. I saw the Rosemary Clark middle school sign on the way to their house. When we arrived at my grandparents' house, my grandfather and grandmother greeted us with open arms. Little did I know that the house would hold many memories for me - both good and bad - for many years. My grandfather showed us the house, and I was smitten.

We drove to a small casino called Terrible Lakeside for dinner. The food was excellent and was better than I thought when I heard about it. After dinner, we drove through the R.V. park behind Terrible Lakeside. It was Christmas time, so the park was decorated with Christmas lights.

The following day, we drove to Las Vegas, which was significant as the last time I visited it was back in 1998. We went to see Mom's friends. Returning from Las Vegas with my Mom and Britney, I saw the lights of Pahrump, and I exclaimed, "We are home!" My Mom replied, "No, we are not."

When my dad arrived in Pahrump on Friday night, grandma showed us around the town. Pahrump was a growing town, popular with seniors. Britney and I got grandma a library and movie store membership card. During that weekend, we surprised the Forrie and Anderson families. Seeing all my aunts, uncles, Grandma Forrie, Bruno, and cousins, especially James and Alyssa, was beautiful. It was indeed a great weekend.

After opening gifts under our first artificial Christmas tree on Christmas day, we spent the rest of the day at Uncle Ray and Aunt Pam's house. Britney and I got into trouble for having a messy room on New Year's Eve. As punishment, our rights to T.V. and movies were revoked. On New Year's Eve, we drove to Julian, California, known for its apple pie. I went to bed. On New Year's Day, I started cleaning my room.

Even though Mrs. Clint was excellent, I did not like Rock Springs Elementary School! I missed all my friends in Portland, and I didn't fit in with the other girls. Only one thing was great: I got to help out in Mrs. Green's special education classroom. The other special education teacher was a cold-hearted lady who always made me cry. My assistant was Mrs. Scotstoun, and I talked to her for a while.

During my time in school, Mrs. Clint had a reading program. When I set my mind to reading each day, I was still reading younger kids' books, and I wasn't at my grade reading level. She will throw a pizza party if we read so many hours a month. She will take our class to a small theme park if we each read beyond so many hours.

Our apartment complex had a handyman named Bobby and its general manager, Sara. In Sara's office, we spent a great deal of time talking. The complex also had a beautiful pool with a breathtaking view of Escondido Valley.

Then the great news came: we were going to Disney California Adventure Park. We would stay at the California Grand Hotel and Spa on my dad's company's dime. When my father told Britney and me, we were so thrilled.

Once we got to downtown Disney, we visited every shop. My parents then went downstairs to a fancy dinner in the ballroom, which had to do with my father's job. It was the first time Britney and I had been alone, and we enjoyed watching whatever we wanted.

In the morning, we rode most of the rides to Disney California Adventure Park. The ride was brand new, not even a month after it had opened, and it was excellent. The whole family loved the ride called 'Soarin over California,' and we rode it twice.

Each week, I had P.T. and O.T. in Vista, California. My mother took Britney and me to the beach after that. We went to Carlsbad's beach. I enjoyed walking on the beach, and it was easy for me. One time, Britney was not with us; my Mom and I were there. We walked barefoot on the sand that day, talking about boys, love, etc. I was fascinated by how people met.

During this time, g had retired from her job. We would visit my grandparents in Pahrump on and off. My grandparents visited me the day after my eleventh birthday, and we went to Wild Animal Park. The day after my eleventh birthday, my grandparents took Britney and me back to Pahrump for a week. Before we went to Pahrump, we saw my Papa's cousin, Tom. He had money and lived in a big, beautiful home that reminded me of Luis Logan's.

Then Uncle Tom showed us around the house. We saw an old picture of someone who looked just like Britney! Britney was amazed to see this. We then discovered that it was my grandmother Murphy, who was twice great-grandmother.

It was a good week in Pahrump. I got stuck in a baby swing and had to call 911. They had to cut me out of the swing! We watched movies, played in the park, got books from the library, and watched movies. My Parents came up just in time for Easter, and the Anderson family came over.

My mother was dissatisfied with me because I was making poor grade marks at school. Britney was doing well in school and getting all "A's ." She was getting all kinds of awards, and she was getting all kinds of stuff done well. With Britney's joy, my Mom bought her toys and bought me a box that had nothing in it. I was sad by this empty box and resolved to work harder.

On a school night, my dad took me to a baseball game. We ate hot dogs, had coke, and cheered for the San Diego Padres. I was so exhausted the following day that I should have stayed home, but I went to school. One of the girls ruined my artwork while I was playing on the whiteboard in Mrs. Green's classroom.

My first time telling someone off was when I let it slip out of my mouth - a terrible word. I got in so much trouble with everyone. I tried to apologize to that girl, but it was too late. I still feel sorry about it today. I am trying to remember why Mrs. Clint wanted to keep me from entering sixth grade. My cerebral palsy. I thought it would be cool to be in the same grade level as Britney, but I wanted to be a year behind. Another year of school? Not for me. I enjoyed school, but now I understand the reason. I wanted to be a writer and to be treated as an equal. People with a disability do not want our malady to hold them back.

It happened, but I ended up in 6th grade. That could be because I read beyond the hours Mrs. Clint set for the reading program. Whichever way it was, I got to go to that small theme park near my house. We played mini-golf, sped around in go-karts, and so on.

The summer before Britney's 10th birthday, I was sick with a high fever and had my first seizure. I don't remember too much about that first seizure. My Mom was helping me out of the bathtub, and then I closed my eyes, and my Mom told me they were open. Suddenly I was able to see again. We had to go to the hospital, and I missed my sister's birthday party after that. Because I hated closing my eyes, I was scared and had to go to the hospital. After that, I had to stay home with my dad, missing my sister's birthday party. I recovered just in time to start middle school at Rincon Middle School in sixth grade.

It was a science summer school, and it was fascinating. Then my dad got another job offer! This time it was back east in Massachusetts. We were all thinking about it. As my parents flew back east, grandma flew into our home to watch us. My Mom and I designed our dream home that we could build in Massachusetts if we moved. My parents had to check out the job there before deciding.

As Britney was already at Rock Springs, I was out for the summer because Rincon Middle School had a twelve-month school year. Grandma, Britney, and I went to school together that weekend since my parents were only gone for one weekend. On that Friday, grandma took Britney to school. We went to Rincon Middle School for its annual school day. I got my class schedule with the organization and met all my new teachers. They also had a B.B.Q. for us to enjoy.

We enjoyed the pool over the weekend, and grandma took us to the mall she used as a teenager. On Sunday, my parents came home, and we watched a funny home movie they made when they were in Massachusetts. Grandma woke me up on my first day at middle school, and my Mom took a picture of me holding my orange backpack, and I started middle school the next day.

We always did some unusual things at Rincon Middle School. Once, they invited professional skateboarders over to do a show for us. I will always remember a professional skateboarder doing handstands professional skateboarders over to do a show for us. I will always remember watching a professional skateboarder do handstands for us. Heather was my full-time aide, and she and I became great friends.

It was time for my parents to decide whether to move back to Massachusetts. I remember my Mom and dad sitting at the little dining room table, and they sent us to our room to talk it over without Britney or me contributing our opinion. Having no idea what would happen, we waited quietly in our room. My parents came into our room. They decided not to move back east but wanted to look for a rental home./

In the morning, my dad called my Mom, telling her to turn on the T.V. right when I was getting ready for school. As I put on my purple socks, I watched the World Trade Center burn down. Yes, it was September 11, 2001. I remember that day at school. Rumors were going around that it would start World War III, and they shut down everything. It was indeed a day that we Americans will never forget.

I met Jane, a girl with a disability who was a year older than me. We used to hang out at her apartment. Her parents divorced but still lived in the same apartment complex. Then, one night when I was sleeping at her house, I noticed something strange. I called my father to come to pick me up.

I asked my parents to let Jane come with Britney and me to a farm later. Those were my mistakes. Jane and Britney had so much in common and spent the day ignoring me. Jane asked me about Britney at school, and I just looked at her and walked away. That was the end of our relationship.

A girl approached me during my lunch one day at school, started talking to me like a baby, and I screamed at her to get out of my face. Grounded again for the weekend and missed beach days, I got after-school detention. (What?) I thought this was unfair as I sat bored in the after-school detention classroom.

The next day in my science class, we had to pick a scientist to do a report on. I chose Diane Fossey to study and to do my report on. I was drawn to her and her powerful story and dressed up as her. I remember I had watched Gorillas in the Mist and fell madly in love with that movie. I got an 'A' on this project.

At this time, my family took day trips to Sea World and The San Diego Zoo. We also stayed in a cute cabin in Big Bear Lake, CA, for three days. We were at the beach every Friday, rain or shine.

As we searched all over Escondido Valley for a home to rent, we also looked at houses by the sea. We found one, but the only problem was that it didn't have air conditioning. My family looked at a stunning house for rent, and we all fell in love with it and put in an offer for it. Life was good. We got the house, but we had to hire a pool man and a landscaper. The owners refused to let my dad do it for unknown reasons, so we did not get it.

We were lucky not to have gotten it since a week later, my Mom, Britney, and I were at the beach. My dad showed up early and asked my Mom and me if we wanted to go to Disneyland.

When I went to school, my dad stayed home looking for work fast, acting as if everything was fine. Then, one day, I came home to find out about the biggest news of my life. We were moving to Pahrump to open our own Forrie Auto Body Shop! Before that, we all had a celebration of the year in California.

We spent that Thanksgiving in Pahrump. I was too sick to see the Forrie Family that Thanksgiving, so I stayed with my grandma and Papa. We had our Thanksgiving dinner at a buffet. My dad stayed behind to look for a house for rent and a building for our business. Even though I wanted to stay in Pahrump and start my new school immediately, my parents told me to get in the car. It was time to say goodbye to our California friends and family. The whole week was sated with dinners with friends! We then packed up and moved. I was thrilled to be living close to my grandma again!

Pre-adolescent Years

My family moved into our new home, a rental in Pahrump. On February 1, 2002, the Forrie family business opened: Forrie's Auto Body (F.A.B.).

I continued 6th grade at the newly-built Rosemary Clark Middle School, my all-time favorite school. To my surprise, there was a cerebral palsy boy named Cody, who was just like me. He walked and talked a little better than I did, but I was overjoyed. At last, I met someone like me, and we became fast friends.

Tammy, who sat right next to me in the homeroom, invited me to her Friday night youth group at her church, and I have fond memories of playing ghost tag one night. Sadly, our family never went to a Sunday sermon at this church.

A few days before the big Valentine's Dance, I took control and asked Cody, and he said yes. We were a famous couple at the dance, and he became my first boyfriend after that. Cody wanted more. Being twelve, I was not even ready for a kiss. He tried to kiss me in the corner of a classroom a few days before school was out for the summer. Yet, I pulled away for some unknown reason, telling him no. Cody got mad at me, and I walked away from him. Now I wish that I had shared my first kiss with him.

My schooling was excellent, and I was getting great grades as I vowed to when I entered middle school. I won an award for a three-page paper, but I still await help. I went before the 6th-grade class to receive that award as my classmates, teachers, Mom, and grandma cheered me on. It sure was breathtakingly incredible.

That summer, I was at my grandparent's house because my Mom now worked full-time by my dad's side, building an empire.

I had fun with Britney to make up for the lost time. I hardly saw her since I was at a different school from her. I was up and on the bus before she was even woken up. I had more homework than she did and was always busy.

I was playing in the blow-up pool in my grandparent's backyard, playing with the newest member of the Forrie family, a puppy named Tucker, and watching Titanic, the 1997 movie, every day. One morning, my cousin James was at my grandparents' house, visiting us all for a week. At first, I was shy and unsure of James because it had been years since I saw him let alone talked to him. James, being ten years older than me, was in college.

Over that week, we had a blast making a brother-sister bond. My Mom's best friend, Maria, came over with her daughter, Tara. Another lifelong friendship formed between Tara and me; to this day, Tara has my back. That was indeed a wonderful summer.

Seventh grade started up. That was my favorite grade of all time. I met my beloved teacher, Ms. Santana, who still calls me her 'dear heart' to this day. She was my special ed teacher, so I had three classes with her. She helped me learn to tell the time and taught me everything I'd never learned. She got me to a better reading level and to tell the truth. She inspired me to become an author when I grew up. She also let me see one of my favorite movies, Ferris Bueller's Day Off.

Sadly, Beth, my all-time favorite aide, wasn't my aide in 7th grade. Someone named Jamie was, and she was pure evil to me when no one was around.

I soon saw the downfall in my home life when my Mom started to abuse me along with Jamie, my aide at school. In my mother's eyes, it seemed like Britney had become the 'Golden Child' overnight. She went to Britney's school awards but not mine. One night, I got mad and told my Mom that she loved Britney more than me. After that was said, my Mom beat me half to death. That's when the abuse – physical and mental – began.

I thought of killing myself one night around Christmas of 2002.

I was so tired of my life. I was under pressure at home and school and lost my friends Tammy and Jenny. Cody wanted more than to hold hands in the schoolyard, but I was not ready. I was missing Jessica and my life in Portland and hating my cerebral palsy and Jamie. I told myself to 'keep going, don't give in.' I have never told a soul until now about my first time coming close to ending my life.

Where was my father, you ask? I hardly saw him at this point in my life. He was working late into the night, a job that was made for two or three people. Dad was dealing with my Mom's anger fits or hiding out in the garage when he was home.

2003 was a great year all around compared to the year before. I was a teenager at last! When I turned thirteen, we had a girls' birthday pool party at Saddle West, a small hotel and casino. We then went to the Palms Movie Theater in Las Vegas. We saw Holes with Shia LaBeouf, one of my teenage heartthrobs, and Sigourney Weaver, my role model.

A new custom home was ready for us to move in at the beginning of summer. I went to a day's summer camp that year, but it was an unhappy time. The smaller kids were unkind, bullying me, so I stopped going.

The immense delight of 2003 was seeing my first real-life Broadway play, The Unsinkable Molly Brown, at Tuacahn in St. George, Utah. The Tuacahn Center for the Arts, located in the mouth of the Padre Canyon, is an outdoor 1920-seat amphitheater that stole my heart. The stage background was striking with the red rocks, Padre Canyon, and a small waterfall.

My Papa's brother, Uncle Jake, and his wife, Aunt Suzie, came for Thanksgiving that year. Also, for Christmas, we got my beloved dog, Bruno, named after my dad's godfather.

2004 was a challenging year. My Mom convinced Britney and me that homeschooling would be amazing, and I fell for her fantastic idea, thinking that it would be awesome to sleep in and that no one would pick on me.

Eighth grade was pure evil. A boy threw a golf ball hard, hitting me right in the middle of my head. Jamie was mentally abusing me, saying I was always no good and would never get into college because I was way too dumb to get in. Not to mention my teacher from hell, Mrs. H., my 8th-grade special ed teacher. It was so hard to leave Ms. Santana's loving classroom setting for Mrs. H's classroom setting. I remember hating all of my cold-hearted teachers. After a disagreement with Mrs. H. and Jamie, one day, my Mom came to pull Britney and me out of Rosemary Clark before Mrs. H. could even write me up for detention, which I did deserve. That's when we started homeschooling, which was a significant mistake in my life.

I turned fourteen with sadness as Peter, the father of my childhood playmate Tiffany, passed away after a car accident. After the memorial, my family had dinner at Bootlegger's restaurant, and we talked about what would happen if my dad passed away.

I remember telling dad that he would live until he was ninety, not knowing that he would never make it to sixty.

Bruno, my dad's godfather, passed away that next August. I had never seen my dad so sad. We took a few days off to relax in St George, Utah. We went fishing, saw Zion National Park, and had day trips out of St. George.

High school was coming now, and my Mom got upset with me after I found homeschooling uncool. I wanted to go to high school; grandma hated the whole homeschooling concept and was very mad at my Mom, giving her a piece of her mind on the day mom pulled us out of Rosemary Clark.

Grandma was the one who helped talk me back into going to high school, yet my Mom got into her head that homeschooling me was best. So, I kissed my high school dreams goodbye and said hello to being lonely with no friends.

My savior from this was a little show called Smallville. For a few months on the T.V. channel A.B.C. Family, they ran ads to start re-showing the show. Now the show was playing new episodes on another T.V. channel, W.B., now known as the C.W. I thought it sounded like a show that was my cup of tea. It was the story of Clark Kent's teenage days before he became the Superman that we all love. I forgot it was already on, yet I watched one episode and did not enjoy it as I'd hoped. Over a month passed when I walked into my living room one day to find Britney watching it. Being bored, I sat down to watch it. From then on, I was hooked on Smallville.

Being a Smallville fan helped me get through the evil parts of my life. Tom Welling is my Superman — well, okay, Lionel Luthor (Lex Luthor's father on the show) had also stolen my heart.

Oddly, over the long, lonely years, I felt like Clark and his gang were my friends with whom I went to high school. Can you blame me? I had no friends to talk to, though James did come over quite often to hang with Britney and me, and he was the one who understood me.

We went to Lake Havasu, Prescott, and the Grand Canyon on Thanksgiving. My parents had spent a few Thanksgiving at Lake Havasu, Arizona, before Britney and I came along. That year they wanted to go back with their daughters to have Thanksgiving dinner at a resort by the water. The resort was very run down, and it wasn't like my parents remembered it. But we had an enjoyable dinner with the sunset on the water.

In honor of Thanksgiving, one of the oldest American holidays, the resort hosts a Thanksgiving buffet in its dining room. A large roasted turkey is served with cranberry sauce, stuffing, mashed potatoes, gravy, corn, green beans, and Brussels sprouts. Dessert included pumpkin pie, cakes, and ice cream.

The next day we drove to Prescott, Arizona, to look at land to build a second home on for when my parents retired since our business was now the best auto body shop in Pahrump. Dad did build his empire, and the money came rolling in, making my Mom happy to be rich.

We fell in love with many lands in an up-and-coming élite homeowner's association (H.O.A.) neighborhood.

That day, I felt so off for the first time in my fourteen years. I was up all night thinking of what my future would be. It turned out that it was my muscle spasms with anxiety/panic attacks. I remember asking my Mom to see a cerebral palsy doctor, and I needed medicine. "You didn't need it when you were a little girl. I would hate it if you have to take medicine for your cerebral palsy now," I recall her saying. I agreed with her. Years later, I learned that I should have been on Baclofen since we discovered I had cerebral palsy. Baclofen, a muscle relaxant, is often prescribed to treat spasticity caused by cerebral palsy.

My relationship with Britney at this point had its ups and downs.

I remember the good times watching her playing video games that I loved, like Kingdom Hearts and Tak: The Power of Juju.

I love her to death. Britney is my sister, my only friend. She was so funny that I'd pee my pants when she made me laugh. Yet, I'd been put in a weird situation with her being treated better than me. Did I resent her? Yes, I did over the years to come.

That Christmas, all my gifts were from Smallville: CD, books, seasons 1 to 3 on DVD, and even a Smallville 2005 calendar. I used that as a poster to hang on my bedroom wall, which looked like any teenage girl's bedroom.

There was a Smallville all-day marathon. From 8 am until 7 pm, Britney's and my eyes fixated on our living room T.V. Ah, the good old days before Netflix binge-watching.

In 2005, Death Valley's desert was blanketed with wildflowers in sporadic bloom, making significant headlines and causing people worldwide to see them for themselves. Being an hour away from Death Valley, California, we'd always go there since my dad loved its golf course. By this time, my father had taken up golf and was surprisingly great at it.

All the big-wigs in Pahrump golfed with him sometimes for business. Most of the time, Britney went golfing with him. Britney was a member of the Pahrump Valley Junior Golf Association. I wanted to join in to golf with my dad because he always worked at F.A.B. For some reason, I was not allowed to learn to play golf.

In the summer of 2005, my Mom and Maria planned the best vacation of my life! By then, Maria was living in Ranchester, Wyoming, and we had a blast. For two weeks, we went to all the grand American landmarks and American National Parks: Yellowstone, Mt. Rushmore, Devil Tower, Crazy Horse, Back Hills, Jackson Hole, and Grand Tetons.

My fond memories of the trip are of staying at Dornan's Cabins Inn in Moose, Wyoming, outside Jackson's Hole. I remember my soul feeling very peaceful there, and I was so happy that I never wanted to leave.

Let's Shake it Up!

To sum up my life from ages fifteen to eighteen, I will switch it up. I was heavily abused and kept away from society during this time frame. Britney was the golden child in my parent's eyes, and she was on the golf team and in the town's leading acting group. She always made headlines in the town's newspaper as a teen and went to high school; unlike me, she was homeschooled.

Britney was a star, bringing home state golf titles with her golf team. She always got the starring roles in plays, yet when Britney was home, she used me as her punching bag. However, I will admit that sometimes I was at fault for the fights.

Britney broke my pinky finger on the day before her fifteenth birthday. I never fully understood why Britney was so horrific on the eve of her birthday. The next day, we happily sang HAPPY BIRTHDAY to her.

The Forrie Auto Body moved to a newly constructed building in 2006 on the town's main Highway 160. My dad had become the C.E.O. of the Pahrump Chamber of Commerce. Everyone knew who Matt, Linda, and Britney Forrie were, yet I was excluded, making me feel like I wasn't necessary.

I remember one time before a school play, my parents were talking to this newspaper reporter, and I just said that I was Amanda, the proud sister of the star.

When we got home, my Mom told me I was an asshole for saying that to the reporter. She went on and on about how I made the reporter uncomfortable. Did I? I shall never know. At this time, I felt like my parents were ashamed of me and my cerebral palsy and tried to hide me in the house. I stayed in the shop's back corner while my parents worked. If you've ever seen the Disney movie Frozen, I was like Elsa. The only time I went out anymore was when we went on trips or vacations or when my Mom took me shopping. Oh, or to see my grandma.

I remember that my grandma would try to sneak me out of my house to drive me around sometimes. We even went to Las Vegas once to shop without my Mom knowing, and my Mom got mad at my grandma when she found out.

Now on to Christmas time, 2006. It would be the last time that I ever saw or spoke to my grandma, Margaret Forrie, again. For personal reasons, I won't go into the details. It was my fault, as well. Not a day goes by that I wish I had done something different. To top this off, my parents started to fight like hell as they did back when we lived in Oregon. My mother told my dad it was either her, Britney, me, or his Forrie family. "I want a divorce" was her new saying.

In the meantime, we had a big, beautiful Sea Ray boat on Lake Mead that we only went out once. On vacation in 2006, we visited Sedona, Arizona. I loved it there. It was a spiritual, magical place, so I set one of my books there. Also inspiring were real-life stories from my Mom and grandma, who owned a sandwich shop set in modern-day Sedona.

While I was growing up, they told me stories about the sandwich shop 'The Sandwich Basket.' My Mom begged grandma to open it with her back when my Mom was just out of high school. It was a mother-and-daughter business.

Britney dropped out of high school in 2008 because she never did any schoolwork. When she got a G.E.D., my parents acted like having a G.E.D. was even better than a High School Diploma. The General Education Development (G.E.D.) tests are a group of four subject tests which, when passed, provide certification that the test-taker has the United States or Canadian high school-level academic skills. It is an alternative to the U.S. High School Diploma, HiSET, and T.A.S.C. test. Yet Britney took her S.A.T. before she got her G.E.D.

I was surprised to find out when I was due to take the S.A.T. I remain upset to this day, and I had no say in this matter a year before Britney's. I got my High School Diploma in the fall of 2008 from a home school program in California, and I graduated with honors on November 5, 2008. Years later in life, I found out that it was "a diploma mill."

At this time, I was very lonely. I had no friends that were my age, and I had dreamt since I was little about going to high school to experience high school life and all its milestones.

Now, there was a kitchenette in the new Forrie Auto Body shop. For ten years, on and off. I came to hate that all-white, windowless, little kitchenette room. It became my little jail cell since I was locked up there from 8 am to 5 pm, or even longer. My family didn't allow me to mingle with customers because they were embarrassed to have a daughter like me.

Writing helped me hugely when I was very lonely. I was authoring short stories, ideas, and plots. Thankfully I wanted to develop a talent for writing at a young age, encouraged by a beloved 7th-grade teacher, Ms. Santana.

I had a deep passion for writing since I had difficulty speaking. I recall jotting down story ideas and plot lines as I grew up. My writing was my sweetest and only way to escape from my home life problems. I became someone else for a while, and I got to fall in love or go on a grand adventure with friends by my side as I faced off with the bad guy. Writing had become my haven, and I survived my loneliness and got what I was feeling out on paper, even my sensual feelings. It was my dream to become an author someday. The sad part of this story is that my sister was dreaming the same idea, wanting to be the next J.K. Rowling. My mother once told me that my sister would be the author of the family, not me.

Indeed, my Mom only read my writings after my sister's book became published and was turned into a major Hollywood movie. It was painful to hear my mother say that. Yet, I pushed on writing and didn't let her stand in my way this time. To this day, Linda has never read any of my books.

One night sitting in the backyard, she asked why I never talked to her anymore, instead just living in my little world. I didn't want to fight, so I told her what she wanted to hear.

One night I wanted to be funny with her. I lay in my bed, put a pillow over my head, and put my hands by my side. I popped up when my Mom walked in. She asked me if I was doing drugs. No way! She was furious. I was mad at what she told me. I would never do drugs. How could I even get drugs when she locked me up? She thought that was beyond my mind because I did not want to do drugs.

All my life and to this very day, I have had a unique bond with my grandma. She was more like a mother to me than a grandma since my mother dropped me off at her house daily.

Grandma raised me to be the woman I am today and taught me everything. She was always there for me, helping and encouraging me to never give up and keep carrying on. I have memories as a little girl of her taking me for ice cream with the top down on her convertible driving. Grandma always told me, "Amanda, you were meant to live an extraordinary life." My Mom detested that I was closer to grandma than her and tried to pit us against each other with mind games.

A side note: In the fall of 2019, during one of my classes at a P.I.P. (the Partners in Policymaking program) training, I learned about I.E.P.s. I learned that I was an 8th-grade dropout and that my homeschooling program was from a diploma mill. I would always pick grandma over here. E.P. that had to do with home life because what goes on in a child's home life can be brought into their school life. Neither the state of Nevada nor the Nye County School District ever once checked in on me. I learned that, homeschooled or not, my I.E.P. should have been revised yearly. Now looking back, where was my M.D.R. too? On my last day of physical school, I had a bad Special Ed teacher. She and my aid had ganged up on me, making me act out. That called for an M.D.R. to occur within ten days, causing a chain of events that might have changed my school and home life. I question the process.

I should have gotten my O.T., P.T., and Speech Therapy and started therapy with a counselor at the high school in Pahrump until I was twenty-two. As soon as I learned this, I became depressed about this newest shocker. Later, my new parents, Ron and Alla, told me they still loved me the same. That it's obsolete since my books are getting outstanding reviews, and I'm passing my P.I.P. class and such. I just added the Nye County School District to my list of people that have done me wrong and moved on.

The Nightmare of Scarlett

My parents had hired my Mom's dear friend, Nancy, to work at F.A.B. helping my Mom out. Nancy had a sister named Scarlett, who was in her 70's.

Scarlett had a married daughter with a significant disability: she was born with no arms or legs and was a wheelchair user. Linda and Nancy thought Scarlett and I would become good friends, and my Mom let Scarlett take me out to the movies, lunches, and such.

My eighteenth birthday was in the vast V.I.P. suite at Red Rock Resort and Casino. It was one of my best birthday parties with many of our family and friends. We had such a blast, acting like we were super-rich V.I.P. members over the weekend.

I only had a 'sleepover' once at Scarlett's house, and it turned out that night was the worst night of my life because she did some unspeakable things to me just after I turned eighteen. Scarlett raped me on the night of April 18, 2008.

Scarlett watched me naked while she was dressed the whole time while I took a bath in her colossal bathtub, taking pictures of me in the nude with her camera. After that, Scarlett wrapped me up in a bath towel, hugged me way too close, kissed my neck, and dried me off. I felt odd about this. Later that night, we spent time together on the bed when Scarlett started kissing my feet and asking me if I slept naked.

It was only in 2021 that I began to recall all the other things that had happened that night. It had been difficult for me to recall them earlier, and it was almost impossible for me to be able to recall them.

Did I tell my parents what she did to me? No, they needed Nancy and someone they could trust working for them. So yes, I hid it.

Since that night, my world has become the worst hell I could imagine. Scarlett mentally abused me every time we were alone. In the fall of 2008, I took my first college class with Scarlett. It was a photography class because I love to take photos and play with them on the computer. That class was no fun at all. I recall my mother had beaten me physically on more than one occasion because Scarlett missed a class, and I failed to email her in deep detail about what we had learned in class.

I felt like my Mom loved Scarlett more than me. Scarlett used to drive me to and from our college class. It was pure torture getting into her truck. I remember grandma was at my house one day when Scarlett came to pick me up. I ran over, trying to get into my grandma's car. I tried to open it but could not! I cried when I got into Scarlett's truck. At the time, I did want to go to college since I dreamed of becoming a librarian and author, and Scarlett laughed it off. She told me that she'd get me into the University of California in Berkeley and pushed me into a business college to do what she demanded of me. Scarlett was now acting like my mother.

While driving to class one morning, I became fed up with her B.S. I blew my cool with her, telling her off. Boy, my butt was in deep hot water when my Mom found out.

I thought about suicide again. I thought that suicide was going to be my end. I wished I had just gone to college, looking back. I know now that the University of California is one of the most highly talked about colleges for disabled people. I ended up only taking a handful of community college classes throughout the years of 2008 to 2011.

I had undergone emotional, mental, and physical abuse from my family. I came to hate Scarlett and didn't know that rape could come in all kinds of forms. I claimed that given my condition and how isolated I was when I was young, being homeschooled and being friendless made me still a child. 2008 to 2010 was pure hell each time.

Nancy had to plan the holidays around Scarlett and me. From when my parents met, Nancy has been my new grandmother, and her husband Vic, my grandfather. Of course, Scarlett was the pure, loving aunt.

My Mom and grandma met Nancy and Scarlett in 2004 through a Red Hat chapter. Yet, I would always need to understand how we became family with Nancy, Vic, and Scarlett. They were never a part of my inner circle by my heart, and God knew how hard I tried to embrace them into the family.

This change resulted in a new family dynamic in our Forrie home. My mother physically abused me because she took Scarlett's side and not mine, sardonically calling me a liar and derogatory names. My Mom or Britney egged me on, pushing me to get mad and then physically abusing me.

They filmed me acting like a crazy woman so they could put me away someday. Wacko-Jacko or the Devil Child were my two new nicknames of mine. Sometimes they even acted like they were on the phone with 911.

In 2009, we bought a second home in Sedona, AZ, and this was where my parents wanted to hang their hats. Our new home was right in the heart of Sedona, and it still sucked in the '70s, a major fixer-upper.

In Sedona, I felt as if my family, whom I loved from my earliest childhood, had suddenly returned to me. It's interesting to think about it now, but they never hit me once there. We went down to Sedona as much as possible while remodeling our "Forever Home." Being in Sedona helped our family return to where we were before we met Scarlett. I began to write my first book, my off-take of The Sandwich Basket, set in modern-day Sedona.

In 2010, Alyssa gave birth to a baby boy, Alex Anderson. Since I was like her little sister, I became Auntie Amanda. To this day, Alex is still my only nephew. Yet, I came to love Alex like he was my son.

April 10, 2010, three days after my 20th birthday. After fighting and taking a beating, my parents did the unthinkable thing. They put me into my dad's truck, and my father drove me to the police department because they refused to believe that Scarlett had done anything wrong. Ultimately, I had to beg my dad not to put me in jail. We ended up taking a long drive to the border of California because I wouldn't get out and go to the beach with my father. I genuinely wish that would have happened.

Nancy messed up Matt and Linda's 30th anniversary? My Mom took me to buy a diamond, but she did not tell my dad. Only I knew. Nancy had gotten the same kind of ring that day before my Mom went to buy it with me. Somehow, I got beat up and had to clean the whole house after, even though I was still sore from the beating. She never blamed Nancy for that, only me.

We fought all summer long. However, my dad was finally able to tell Scarlett off, telling her to leave the shop. After that, Scarlett marched into the shop to tell my dad that she would take me away for the weekend to look at college.

A Man name Scott

In the fall of 2010, I was a part-time college student working on "Wildflower," my first novel. As a volunteer, I volunteered at the Pahrump Community Library, which I loved. In 2008, Ally, a librarian, got me my job at Pahrump Community Library. This library became my haven, and I am still in shock at my mother for leaving me alone during her watch. At that library, I met Scott, and we became friends.

.My Mom had been fighting with me for quite some time about Scarlett. I freaked out when I found out Scarlett was trying to convince me to be alone. I had no idea what to say or whom to turn to for help. I had developed a condition known as Genuphobia. Yes, it is a real thing. As a result, I gave Scott what I had written on my computer and let him read it for a while one day. After 20 minutes, Scott looked at me with a tear running down his cheek. He told me, "Amanda, Scarlett has raped you," and I was confused but relieved at the same time.

The feeling was strange. Scott explained everything to me, even sharing his own rape story that I will not share, He wanted to put her in jail, but she waited until after I was eighteen, so he couldn't do a thing. Scarlett's front door would have been a perfect place for Scott to knock.

Scott offered assistance when someone picked me up. "YES!" I thought my mother would beat me if I told her this.

Rather than grandma, my Mom picked me up this day. With Scott's help, I told Linda everything that had happened to me. She was very upset about what Scarlett had done to me. My life; totally changed! A woman had raped learning I radically changed my life. Scott told Linda and me to get rid of anything that made me think of Scarlett, write a letter to her about how much pain she had caused m, and then set it on fire.

I remember, after that, saying my goodbyes and thank you to Scott. Meeting his eyes, I felt like something hit me deep inside my soul, a strong spiritual bond between us. I had never had this strong feeling about a man before or after.

The next time I confided To Scott was the day after I lost my temper in the college computer lab. I was working on my homework, and these two women didn't know I was within earshot. They started talking smack about my Mother and baby sister, making me mad. They were my family, good or bad. I melted down, losing my temper in the middle of the computer lab. I let them have it. Britney and I agreed not to tell our parents. I spelled it all out, crying to Scott and Ally. "There is something wrong with me!" We chat about it.

Yet when I saw my mom, she was in tears. "You stood up for me, Amanda?" my mom asked. Then my mom finally confessed that she had been talking to Nancy. Nancy told my mom that Scarlett invited the whole family to dine with them at one of the top restaurants in Las Vegas. Then my mom got peeved and told Nancy what her sister did to me. When Scott and I heard this from my mom, I saw him crying. Seeing him crying, I cried with him. That's when I knew I had feelings for him.

During this time, I saw my father's health go downhill fast. He stayed home, extremely ill. We thought it was just bad food poisoning, yet it lasted much longer than food poisoning. Three weeks passed, and he was still suffering. We all couldn't understand what was going on with dad. Dad refused to see a doctor since he hated all doctors.

"Is dad dying, mom?" I asked once, and she just called me out on it.

My Beloved Father

One morning, my dad woke up in so much pain that we rushed him to an E.R. in Las Vegas. On November 11, 2010, he had surgery. I recall my Uncle Chuck being with us all day until he had a meeting, but he came right back after. I have forgotten what the doctors diagnosed my dad had.

We all followed my dad until they wheeled him into the surgery room. I was terrified, with tears in my eyes. The surgery did not even last two hours. My mom, Britney, and I went to lunch late. Before we got our food, we had to dash out because the doctor called and needed to talk to all of us.

When we returned, a doctor met us in the hospital lobby and asked us to follow him. I just knew the 'death news' was coming. We were in this tiny room, and the door closed as he told us that my dad was dying of stage 4 cancer. He told us to get everything in order and say our goodbyes to Matt Forrie. I almost passed out in that damn room and cried my heart out all night. After hearing the news, Jessica called my Mother's cell phone the following day. I loved hearing her voice. My dad had been so upset that they told his two young daughters before him.

After that, we called Grandma Forrie on speaker but got her voicemail. My dad told mom, "Do not tell my mom that I'm dying on a voice message." We all knew why dad said this. Recently we lost my dad's brother Uncle Kenny, my favorite uncle. Uncle Kenny always had a huge smile and a bigger heart. He was a teddy bear of a man.

We were blessed that my dad got to come back home the day before Thanksgiving Day. While it was a far cry from our Thanksgiving on Lake Havasu, it was special. Dad got to continue to stay home thanks to months of home care.

I dropped out of college to be my dad's caregiver. I shall never regret taking care of my father. Britney had to take over F.A.B. and work there when she was not at college. It was hard. I took care of my dad daily, which is how I got addicted to Facebook. After a long time of bugging my parents to get on Facebook. Britney had her Facebook account, so I wanted mine. I just fell in love with talking and catching up with wonderful old friends from Portland.

In the meantime, Scott had become a close friend to me. He helped me deal with everything that was happening. At that moment, my mom and Britney teased me about having a girl crush on Scott at school. Scott was older than me, but I didn't care, wondering if he would love someone with cerebral palsy like me.

My 21st birthday was just dear to me. I didn't want to do what I had planned with mom and Ally: a night of drinking my butt off. It was to be "The Ultimate Girls' Night Out," which included a Chippendale's show with song, dance, and striptease. We went to a jazz bar; Tommy Jensen owned it and was there that night. Tommy came up to me, recalling the baby girl who sat on his lap while his commercial was being filmed. He couldn't believe that this little girl was now 21 and that he was serving me my first drink. It was extraordinary. It felt like my dad had called Tommy explicitly, asking if he could be there because he couldn't.

During this time, I was thankful for Jessica and Scott. I can't tell you how much they helped me deal with my new life when dad went on a journey to Kindred Hospital, which offered in-depth care for him. Grandpa Forrie and Aunt Naomi were by his side. In my dad's absence, my Grandpa Forrie was there for him. I remember him being there only for his son, and that's about all I recall. Rather than being my birth grandpa, he behaved like a step-grandpa to me.

My mom went into road rage on our drive when a car cut her off. She got furious at the people in the other vehicle, yelling and following their car. My sister and I had to beg her to stop! The other driver kept blowing kisses at her, provoking her to hit their car. That's when I knew that she could easily talk about life.

I hate thinking that I had to live with her without my dad. I can't say what I thought or felt as dad got to the end. He moved onward to Nathan Adelson Hospice for end-of-life care. We spent r two whole sleepless weeks waiting for that call.

As I recall the last time I saw my dad before we went to Scott's house for dinner, the pain of this memory is too sorrowful for me to put down into words. Let's say when I saw Scott, he hugged me as I cried.

After eight months and eleven days, my beloved father went to Heaven on July 22, 2011, seven months after Grandma Forrie passed. It was a significant loss.

My mom would not even hold a memorial service for my father. After everyone got onto her to have some memorial service, Linda gave in, saying there would be a Life Celebration to relive the many happy memories. On Saturday, July 30, at 2:00 P.M. at Mountain Falls Golf Club, Pahrump, NV. Over 100 friends and relatives brought their remembrances of my father.

Jessica flew in to be with me in my time of need for four days of fun. After all, we had just turned twenty-one. While Jessica was with me, she met Scott and my family.

Then one night, I confessed to Jessica that I had romantic feelings for Scott. She tried to make sense of it to me, and she didn't think it was right. And that's when I told her what Scarlett had done to me.

After Jessica left, we went somewhere in Utah to spread my father's ashes and say farewell to him. It was beautiful, and I knew in my heart that he was happy in his resting place.

Life without Dad

I was devastated by my dad's quick death, and I bought a book and a program on how to write a screenplay because I needed something I had never done before to take my mind off my father's death. I locked myself in my room (in a way) for a month to learn and wrote "Pit Boss." My mom was a mess, and I was terrified of what she would do next. Kill me with her new toy, a gun?

Britney was now running our business. She was mad at the world because going to college was not in the cards for her now.

I never understood why Britney could be whatever she wanted to be in life. Britney wanted to be a best-selling author; I did too.

We hired a man to help run the shop. His name was "Al," short for Allen. His wife Eva was our housekeeper. All of our lives changed when we met Al and Eva. My Mother was more accepting, and we temporally got along.

Now that I was more out in public, I continued to see Scott and even started going to lunch and hanging out with him.

We learned Al had grown up as a mobster's son in Buffalo, New York. Al and his wife took us three under their wings and ensured we all had fun together on the weekend in Las Vegas. We went to nice dinners, went shopping, and drove out to Lake Mead. Al helped me with my many Mafia questions. By now, I had become obsessed with the Mafia. Strangely, I remember Al telling me about knowing Joe Fino.

Britney and I saw the Lion King on Broadway, driving her new red 2003 T-bird.

All that stopped when Nancy got very jealous of Al and Eva. After Vic died, Nancy took mom to California. When my mom got back, she turned back to her evil ways, telling Scott that we were done with him and firing Al for some dumb reason. She wanted me to stop saying that Scarlett raped me because she didn't rape me.

It was such an awful night in 2012. I came so close to death as I said my last prayer, and I thought I saw the light at the end as I prayed. During the time Britney cheered on her to murder me, my mom nearly killed me and locked me up in our house once more. It was only a handful of Facebook friends with whom she approved that I was able to speak. As a result, my Mother ensured Jessica and Scott had to go.

After a year, I still had a hard time grieving the loss of my father and trying to find footing in my new life.

In the summer of 2010, my grandma took me to a tiny movie rental store. It had a small collection of movies, and one caught my eye. It was Casino starring Robert De Niro, Joe Pesci, and Sharon Stone. I remember watching a part of Casino on T.V. a few months prior while waiting for one of my favorite shows, Big Love, to come on. Well, for some reason, we never returned to Casino. I always wanted to watch it all the way through. I then asked my grandma if we could rent it, and she told me we could since I was twenty. So that night, we made Mexican tacos and put on Casino to watch. I became very interested in the movie when I saw that it was based on actual events. I know it was acting, but I was scared of that one guy who killed everyone at the end, and that night I ended up sleeping with my grandma. The next day, I woke up wanting to learn more about Casino and the real story. I started to investigate it. I quickly forgot about it due to my life drama. Then something unique happened! It was a turning point in my life!

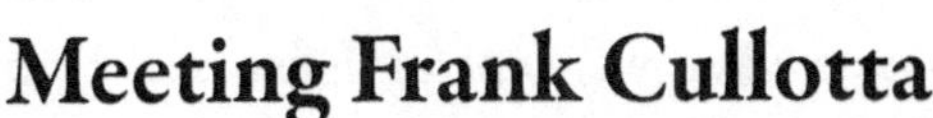

Meeting Frank Cullotta

For my twenty-second birthday, I decided to go to the newly-opened mob museum. Little did I know, I was about to meet someone who would play a significant role in helping me with "Omerta Affair," another of my books.

A few days before I went to the mob museum, I went on the museum's website to see if some event was going to take place while I was there. I found out that Frank Cullotta would be there signing his book. Cullotta would be there at the same time as I was going to be there! Now at the time,

I only found out who he was when I looked up his name on Wikipedia. The character of Frank Marino in Casino was based on Frank Cullotta; I got excited! I always thought it would be very cool to meet a real-life ex-mobster.

When my party arrived at the museum, a family member of mine told the parking attendant that it was my birthday. The parking attendant wished me a happy birthday, and he let us in to park. Out of the corner of my eye, I saw the parking attendant get on his walkie-talkie. After we parked the car, the parking attendant approached me and told me to go into the gift shop because Frank Cullotta was waiting for me to wish me a happy birthday.

I could not believe my luck. Maybe this parking attendant was full of it. To this day, I still don't know! We went in and waited for some friends to show up while we got our tickets. I got in for free — it was my birthday, after all. In the gift shop entryway, there was a sign saying that Frank Cullotta was signing his book. A friend of mine took a picture of me by the poster when we went in. I first saw Frank sitting there, signing his books and taking pictures.

There was a long line to meet him. We decided to look around the shop until the line went down. After a bit, there was no line. I walked up and stood behind the person who was having their copy of Frank's book signed by him. After that person was done, I thought I was next to meet Frank. I started to walk up to him, but it turned out that the man next to me was there before me and was following. That could have been the more comfortable situation. I let the man go ahead and waited for my turn.

When I finally met Frank, he stood up and shook my hand. Then Frank asked me if I wanted a picture with him, and I said, "Sure," so we took one, but for some reason, it didn't turn out, so we took another one. To my surprise, Frank hugged me as the picture was being taken. After that, Frank and I started talking about his life and my desire to write. I told him I was a writer working on my first book about the Mafia. He was interested and gave me a free picture of us since; it was my birthday. He even signed it for me. Afterward, we wished each other goodbye, and I went into the museum with my party. Little did I know I would see Frank again,

I went to a bookstore for three weeks, bought Frank's book Cullotta, and read it. After I'd finished the book, I wondered, what if he was on Facebook?

I found his Facebook fan page and got up the courage to message him telling him who I was and that I'd enjoyed his book and meeting him. A couple of days later, he replied to my message, which is how our friendship began. And with Frank's help, I became an author at last!

In September of 2012, I was in my room and had a crazy idea to write a Casino fanfic. I planned to have Nicky's son and Ginger's daughter discovers that their parents, Nicky and Ginger, were star-crossed lovers, leading them to the past.

All of my family and friends love it! That was when I decided to take what I already wrote off a fanfic site and continue my story, renaming every person and turning it into my novel. I finished it and had it professionally edited.

When it was all done, it went out for sale on Amazon.com. I was jumping with joy. It was a super, fantastic, wonderful feeling! "I did it. I am a published author!" I made my dream come true!

At home, one day, my mom took Scarlett's side and told me that Scarlett was a dear mother and grandmother who loved her late husband and would not do those things to me. She said that I had made everything up with my buddy Scott. My mom and I went back to fighting a lot.

My mom verbally, mentally, and physically abused me. I am not an angel, and I have my demons.

I have a temper, a horrible temper sometimes. I truly egged on my mom and Britney because what life did I even have? Mom forbade me to even date any guys at ages 22 and 23. Yet Britney sure did date. Years later, I was talking to my grandma, who told me my Mother put a lot of that anger and hate inside me when I was young. My mom never entirely accepted my cerebral palsy and never really had the time or wanted to embrace my condition. I genuinely know that my temper played a significant part in her lack of acceptance.

As I was growing up, she made me believe that I was a terrible whack job and that the only side effects of my cerebral palsy were my slowness of walking and talking. My mom told me I should not hang out with other disabled kids, and I felt like she was ashamed and hated me because I had cerebral palsy and was not perfect.

Yet it did not stop me from writing and publishing my first book, a mafia romance. It's hard to believe that Frank Cullotta took someone like me under his wing and invited me to everything.

In 2013, Frank held a Mob-Con. It was a three-day event to meet real mobsters, law enforcement officers who put them away, and speakers and crime authors like me selling their books. Not every day do you see mobsters, F.B.I., C.I.A., news reporters, and actual crime authors all in one ballroom talking about the good old days and acting like old friends. Going to a Mob-Con changed my life for the better. I met someone who changed my whole life.

They threw the V.I.P. cocktail party the night before Mob-Con started and held at the Mob Attraction at the Tropicana. I was super early, the first at the party, along with my mom and grandma.

When we entered the room, I noticed a man was already there. He walked up and started talking to me as if he'd known me my whole life. He explained that his name was Ronald Fino. Ronald was one of the F.B.I.'s foremost undercover operatives who worked in Russia. His wife, Alla, was Russian. I told Ron all about myself and my new book. His face lit up.

He said to me that he would call me Sasha. He took a picture of us together. Writing about this memory fills my heart with joy. Little did I know I'd just met my beloved 'daddy.'

Mob-Con 2013 holds a dear place in my heart. I met my wonderful friends Peter Scharff, Gary Jenkins, and Dennis N. Griffin and hung out with Frank, whom I love like an uncle; he let me call him Uncle Frank now.

Thinking back on it, how I wish I could have gone home with Ron after Mob-Con 2013 and avoided the hurricane that was about to come and its dark aftermath.

Anderson Family War

Right after Mob-Con, my mom turned into a different person. She was always fighting with me, my grandparents, and my Uncle Chuck, who dropped what he was doing to help us when we discovered that my father was dying. We had our horse at his ranch that we went to each weekend at the base of Mt. Charleston, Nevada. Uncle Chuck had been the one who found Al and did so much more.

Britney was dating a guy who worked at F.A.B., which my mom did not like. Britney and mom were always at it too. Who was this woman that I called my mom for twenty-three years?

In 2014 after a violent outburst between my mom and Britney, Britney and I just had it with her. I followed Britney, got into her car, and drove off, making a plan with Uncle Chuck.

We planned to get our pad in Las Vegas and start living away from our Mother, dearest. I was tired of living under her thumb and felt like I was in the jail my mom had made for me. She was always looking at my Facebook, emails, texts, and everything, opening and reading my mail after I was over eighteen. If she didn't like a friend of mine on Facebook, she made me block or unfriend them. She made me turn my back even on Jessica.

It is damn sad that Britney and I went to meet our mom at our spot in Red Rock Canyon at twilight after two days of not speaking with her. I begged my sister with tears not to go to Red Rock. However, Britney did it at last. I felt heartbroken and betrayed by my baby sister as we met with mom. My Mother's words now brainwashed Britney. Yet, I did not fall for her bull-brainwashed lies, and I pretended to. What choice did I have? It wasn't like I could drive away on my own.

Two weeks after our talk, I never wanted to see my mom's face again. It was the night of what would have been my father's fifty-ninth birthday — if he were alive, and we were talking. We were not even drinking. My mom honestly confessed and admitted that she hated me since she discovered I had cerebral palsy. I was heartbroken and knew I had to run away the following day. I wrote a note that read: "The Wacko has left," and put it next to a picture of the three of us.

On that very same day, I saw Scarlett at last. She came up to my grandma and me at Walmart, hugging grandma. I was so afraid of death that I ran as fast as possible out of Walmart and fell. That was in February 2014, the last time I saw Scarlett. Walmart almost called the cops on Scarlett, not me.

My Mom, Linda, took Scarlett's side, telling me that the cops should have come for me, not Scarlett. My mom and I fought over the phone that night, and I wish Scarlett had killed me after she raped me because living with it is very hard, even to this day.

After that, I lived with my grandma and my Papa at their home. I started seeing Scott aging because my grandparents always liked him around me. I learned that my mom was getting ready to send me far away, somewhere in Texas. My grandparents were thankful I ran away before she locked me up and forgot about me for good.

I got back in touch with Jessica after not having her in my life for over a year. She had just picked up the keys to her new house on the same day. She was set to marry that summer. Jessica was so happy because she never felt right about having a life without me. I reconciled with my Aunt Tammy, Naomi, and Aunt Linda on Facebook.

Alex, my only nephew, was my joy because he got me through my first holidays alone. Now that I had grown up knowing lies, I felt like my childhood was a lie. All the made-up stories about my family members were a lie. Lie. Lie. It is time for me to begin building my own life at age 23, without my mom and Britney.

Our Romance Story

My first real kiss was with Ray, who was well over sixty-five, and it makes me disgusted at the very thought of it to this day. Ray was my next-door neighbor. I was spending time with Ray, fixing a computer, talking about this and that, and I was alone with him at his house. Then Ray started asking me sexual questions. Then he told me: "I want to make love to you!" I was shocked by this since I was twenty-three and had never been kissed before by a man, let alone had sex. He convinced me he was the only man who would sleep with me.

I almost came close to having sex with Ray on that day. What was I holding out for a Prince Charming? a Jack from the movie Titanic? Or even Scott? He said he was the only man who would want to have sex with me. Luckily, he couldn't get it up and egged me into kissing him. If Ray had gotten hard, I would have done it with him that day to know what sex was.

After I said no thanks to Ray, he took me home. My grandparents were distraught when I told them about it, and we didn't dare call 911 because my mom would have taken the chance to take me away from them.

Upon telling Scott what happened, he helped me realize how valuable I was to him. It was now or never to let Scott know my romantic feelings. I wrote him a love letter and gave it to him to read. When Scott was reading, I expected he would laugh and say we were good friends since his son was here. When Scott changed the mood between us, a new light appeared in his eyes. He then declared his love for me, leading to passionate kisses.

We started dating, and It was the best time of my life being with him. Scott took me to the Pahrump Valley Wine for our very first date. The first time I had a sexual experience with Scott, I shall never regret that experience. He made me feel so beautiful and pure that I can shed a tear of joy even as I write this down as I remember it.

I finally found a counselor to help me deal with my childhood trauma. Her name was Heidi. I even got an unusual social worker named Kitty. The truth is, Kitty became one of my closest friends. Please do not ask me why, but my best relationships/friendships always seem to be with people far older than me. I have a good relationships with people far older than me. Kitty and I had this fantastic friendship where we could tell each other anything. We were always together, running around the town. I even wanted her to be one of my bridesmaids If Scott asked me to marry him. Due to unforeseen circumstances, she is not in my life anymore.

Scott and I were having a love affair with lunch dates, and we wrote love letters to each other. I felt so loved when I was with him; he was my great love and soul mate.

It was Good Friday in 2015, and Scott and I had a fun time eating the Jimmy John's subs that he had surprised me with while we played war, my favorite card game that no one had ever bet me on until this day. He won. The romantic atmosphere between us led us to plan an official date to go to Red Rock Casino, Resort, and Spa, as we had previously discussed. We planned it for a date in May as my birthday gift. My 25th family birthday party would be on April 19, and he would also attend. Scott has a 12-year-old son living with him, and he alleged that his ex-wife, who lives in Colorado, told him that she would get full custody of their son, stating she was a heartless soul. She would use in court that because of my cerebral palsy and was the same age as their oldest son.

I understood that he did not want to lose the chance of losing custody because of my having Cerebral Palsy Scott and I were heartbroken, and we did talk about getting married one day.

That I fell into a deep depression, I was angry at the whole world and even at God, hating and blaming everyone. I did not want to kill myself. Against my will, I stayed at Seven Hills Behavioral Health Hospital, a psychiatric hospital, for a week. I owe it to Heidi, my counselor, who back-stabbed me along with a new social worker named June. June did the sending me away, I learned later. Still, I didn't understand it in 2015. Locked up at Seven Hills was hard for me. I didn't bathe because the shower's knob was so hard, and I didn't want to let another woman ever see me naked. My worst nightmare is coming true. My doctor played God with my life, making me stay put for as long as the law allowed her, telling me that I was homeless and had no place to go. Seven Hills wasn't disability-friendly. They wouldn't let me cry alone in my sadness, either. They said they would keep me for another week if I did not straighten up.

My grandma fought tooth and nail to get me back home after seeing me in such poor health. My Grandparents got mad at whoever told me that they had kicked me out of their home. My grandparents and I ran out of Seven Hills as fast as they could get me free, yet it didn't last too long.

Hello, my Dear Mother

Side note: I will use my natural Mother's name, Linda, and I will not call her my mom.

A year and a half went by; I only had contact with Linda in July 2015, when we each agreed to fix our mother/daughter relationship with the help of Heidi and my social worker, June. By this time, I was ready to get my apartment to be independent. My grandpa was getting old and needed much help and care from my grandma. Equally, my lousy behavior and temper would be too much for her.

She did not need that added stress. Linda helped me find my pad and helped move me in and set me up in my new apartment. She was getting me a dog helped too.

I was getting along with Britney, and Britney and I were working out our issues.

Yet my chances of reconciliation with Britney were way higher than my chances with Linda. Linda promised me that she or Britney would always come over, and I believed that Linda had changed. She was the ever-loving Mother I needed, sucking me into thinking she would be an excellent mother. Previously it had only been a brief time until she showed her actual colors.

The whole apartment and living on my idea was a big mistake. Scott also has to take a second job. I was so very lonely. No one popped in to see me except grandma, who came almost every day. Linda had turned back to her old self. She'd just come over to yell at me or give me bull about this and that if she did come over. Linda and Britney forbade me from setting foot in their home like I was taboo. I couldn't even go up to see my beloved cats and dogs that I loved. They always give me a questionable reason. I wanted to return to Seven Hills because it was way better than living there.

Scott and I were still going out, Skyping, and texting daily. Heidi bowed as my counselor because she had found a new job out of state. After Heidi, I ended up getting the evilest counselor of my life. Leading to having a big meeting in Heidi's office with everyone ready to haul me off to a mental hospital for my whole life or put me in a group home. Linda told them then that she would look for a group home for me, and we walked out of that meeting,

Afterward, Linda made it clear that she wasn't looking for a home to, as she put it, "put your butt in." I ended up drinking wine all day each day for over a month. Grandma was heartbroken to see me become a heavy drinker, and she begged Scott, Linda, and Britney to help clean me up. So, Linda stepped in and helped me, for which I am grateful.

* * *

On the morning of December 15, 2015, 5, After a sleepless night with mean texting from Linda back and forth, she told me that she would disown me and that I needed to go and kill myself. She said I was a useless drunk with a lousy temper and outbursts in public when someone treated me like a baby or made fun of me. She said I was a monster that needed to die.

I felt like I had just lost Linda and my sister. I felt like Scott did not love me anymore, and I couldn't write anymore. Some people viewed me like there was some evil within me. I had nothing left to live for in my life. I was all alone in the world. I was emotionally done! I just wanted to see my daddy and be with him.

I attempted suicide by taking all my prescribed medication. I had called grandma to say goodbye and that I loved her, wishing her all the best in her life. I took a bath, ready to fall asleep in the water. After a while, I got out of the tub and sat there half-naked, praying to go.

Linda and her friend rushed me to the E.R. to save me. Linda and grandma were with me the whole time, not talking to each other after I'd begged them to stop fighting; I guess God did not want to take me to Heaven yet.

For a few days, I couldn't walk and barely talk. They all told me that I would never talk or walk again. I was upset that Linda saved my life and just told me she wished me to die. I remember Linda and Scott came to see me in a psychiatric hospital, and I was crying when I told them how much I loved them. It was hard to look at and talk to Linda and Scott — there were so many mixed emotions. I recalled a better time in my life, picnics in the park with Scott.

We even agreed that we had to have been husband and wife in our past lives. He just looked at me and told me that he loved me.

As we entered 2016, we all discussed that living alone was not the most fabulous idea. I had to give in, so I moved back home under my Mother's roof until Linda found a group home. Linda and Britney reminded me that I was like a renter. There was no way that this was my home since I ran away. I was brainwashed once more into believing that a group home was the place for me.

We had planned to go to Flagstaff, Arizona, for a weekend getaway. Linda messed up everything between us, leading me to break up with him.

I never sent the actual goodbye letter to Scott, all thanks to Linda. Things got terrible once more between Linda and me too. One day while chatting with Jessica, she told me I needed to devise a plan B. Anything would be better than being a number in a group home. I sat on it and wondered who would take me in. I had started to chat with Ronald Fino, whom I had met at Mob-Con, especially since my O.D. attempt. We had even spent time together when Frank put on another Mob-Con in 2014. Ron had his twenty-year-old son, Daniil, with him, whom I liked. I was thinking about flying to see Ron and having a break from my world before I moved to a group home and gave up my freedom.

Flying to Williamsburg

Looking back, in 2016, I am not proud of myself, and I am very ashamed of my injurious behavior and temper. After another disagreement with Linda, we had yet another nasty fight leading up to me hitting my mom. I was kicked out with nowhere to go. Before reaching out to Ron, I called my whole Forrie-Anderson family and Frank and Scott.

I immediately flew out there without a thought since I had to give a quick, last-minute answer. Nevada social services called Ron Fino to ask if he could help me. After calling various assistance groups near where I was still waiting. Ron and his family said they would take me in. It was time for a new start in my life and to get far, far, far away from Linda. The first summer, Ron took me to Virginia Beach. Thinking that Virginia Beach was just like Carlsbad Beach in California, I lost my footing in the sea, and my dad had to save my life that day. I would be gone if he acted more slowly than he did. I've always loved the 4th of July as my second favorite Holiday. Ron and Alla took me downtown to Colonial Williamsburg for the first time.

We took the time to stroll down the most historic thoroughfare, Duke of Gloucester Street. It was just like returning to the very first 4th of July. The firework show blew my mind away, and it was the best fireworks show I have ever seen.

Hollywood then came knocking. My future dad's book, Mr. Undercover, was being made into a documentary. They came into our home for a week to film it in June 2017. I have a part in it! I acted like dad had just come home as my mom, and I came to greet him with our two dogs: Ash, a black lab, and Milia, my purebred German Shepherd. Filming Mr. Undercover was also a blast, and it was exciting to be part of the documentary.

I was fascinated to learn the ins and outs of making it and shocked to see a clip of Nicholas Pileggi talking about Ron's movie. I was also shocked when I learned that Robert De Niro was a good friend of my Ron.

Ronald and Alla are my soul parents. We had lots of fights along the rugged, rocky way. Together, dad and Alla made me a better person, helping me to chase my demons away with the power of love. I owe my life to them for saving me in so many ways. My friend once told me that my eyes always light up when discussing my future dad.

My only regret is not revealing to my new family everything about my past. I was too dumb to think I could hide my past and start a new life, just like in a movie.

At first, I was an absolute hell's angel. Once I got to Williamsburg, I signed up for online dating and began going out with men I met on dating sites. I was trying to find a husband as quickly as possible, so I would not be a freeloader.

I was going to marry a man whom I found out was a con artist who was in the army. I also had numerous temper tantrums and outbursts with Ron and Alla, which was disrespectful to them due to my upbringing. It took me years to stop my wicked ways. I got back in touch with Scott since he never wanted to break up with me, and we Skyped each week, having a long-distance relationship. I wasted my money on a psychic cult on Facebook who saw me getting back together with Scott and giving birth to our daughter.

I bought whatever I wanted. I was no angel to dad or Alla and always fought with them. I even hit them. I also once asked a family friend to drive me to hook up with a guy. It took us years to form this genuinely magnificent family relationship. I do not know how dad and Alla keep me around for so long, thinking back on it.

A.D.F. of Williamsburg

I started going to the Adults with Disability Friends (A.D.F.). The A.D.F. of Williamsburg is a group of parents of adult children with disabilities. Who got together on behalf of and served people with intellectual and developmental disabilities. I was so thrilled to be one of the members of the A.D.F. of Williamsburg.

I was busy at the A.D.F. and always went to sporting events like basketball, baseball, and car racing. I also did the one-mile walk for the A.D.F. 5k! We were very involved with the community and the outstanding college students at the College of William and Mary in Williamsburg. I wanted to avoid joining the A.D.F. in the first place! The first week I moved here, my dad wanted me to sign up for the A.D.F., and I said no because, at that time in my life, I had not accepted my cerebral palsy entirely.

Some time went by before I finally gave in at last. Dad took me to meet Mary, the A.D.F. leader, at her house. I grew fond of Mary. Boy, I wish that I had never made friends with a girl named Ashley at the ADF. in late summer of 2018. She was the daughter of one of the founding families of the A.D.F. I started talking to Ashley each morning on Facebook. It was terrific at first. Then Ashley began treating me as if I were dumb. She was very selfish and manipulated me. She only wanted to talk about herself.

She would brush it off when I tried to tell her what I was doing. When I finally said something about it, I felt like Ashley made it about her or made it into a competition. She would turn my words and my feelings into her own. She would text me before 6 A.M. every day. Some days, Ashley made me cry or got me in a foul mood.

We rode the same bus, and she always sat next to me. Once Ashley told me to shut up five times when I was trying to get into a conversation with her. I tried to stop talking to Ashley many times on Facebook, but it never worked. I wanted peace in the A.D.F. and on the bus. I did not want more drama. It got to the point that I had to block Ashley on Facebook after I tried to end our friendship gently, and she egged me on into a fight. I kept away from her the next day at a P.J. movie party. Still, when the movie started (Lilo & Stitch), she started bullying me, calling me crazy, and giving me an evil look. Without a word, I walked out and went into the other room. She called our friends before the party and told them something about me. It felt like everyone was shunning me!

I was a royal mess and hit rock bottom. I reflected on my latest mistake, turning around in my computer chair to see a cold, cloudy day. By my computer was the letter from the Adults with Disability Friends, telling me I was no longer welcome or fit to be a member because of my anger outbursts that upset the others.

It is hard to say, but I have a severe anger problem, and sometimes I get mad trying to stand up for my and my friends' rights.

At a bowling alley one summer night, we all were made to drink water, and they would not let us buy what we wanted to drink or even what we wanted to eat and told the people who worked there not to take our hard-earned money.

I felt like they were playing God with us disabled people. That is why I got so upset! The guy I was trying to hook up with dumped me. I had always cared for him, but he was getting back with his ex, and I had to see them together.

One night in January 2019, I had a lousy outburst after they denied me the right to call my dad and go home after being shunned by the whole group. I begged to call my dad, trying to use my cell phone. I felt frightened, but they wouldn't let me do something safe for everyone. I tried to walk out, but it caused a significant scene, like when I was eight. It was not pretty.

I thought about Jessica, wondering if she was at home. Was she making dinner for her husband and their children? I was, feeling like that same Amanda, still an eight-year-old school girl while Jessica was at home playing with her children and being a loving wife.

For a while, I'd been bullied by my so-called friends, and I ended up often sitting alone at A.D.F. dances and such. A female volunteer drove me nuts trying to be my friend. Let's say that there was something odd about her that rubbed me the wrong way.

Finding too much drama at the A.D.F., I went home and took it out on my parents. I began fighting with them because I began to dislike the A.D.F.

Looking back, I regret what I did. I was not an angel sometimes. I do apologize to all of the leaders of the A.D.F. of Williamsburg.

Ashley went right after another new girl in the group, Kit. Kit reached out to me, telling me how nasty Ashley was to her, saying she was driving her crazy. Like she did with me, Kit wanted to start drinking and begging me for help. I told Kit that my hands were tied and I was sorry. After two months of not going to the A.D.F., I told Mary I was sorry and that we could work it out.

On March 4, 2019, I received a letter. Because of my temper, that said: I would not be welcome in the A.D.F. It's not the worst thing I ever did in Williamsburg, either, but it was terrible.

In May 2017, I woke up in the I.C.U. at the hospital with no memory of overdosing on my medication and trying to commit suicide. I remembered I had to end it for good with Scott, and I was so much pain over it.

When Scott and I broke up, my mom threw me out; I moved in with the Fino family. Scott won't lose his son to his ex-wife. We tried to have a long-distance relationship, but it was not to be.

I felt like something in my soul had died. I felt like I had lost my whole family. Why go on living? All I can tell you is that I was on my computer one minute, and the next moment, I was waking up in the I.C.U. a few days later. I was close to death. It was my dad and my mom who saved my life. I was now back in a psychiatric hospital in Hampton, Virginia. While I was there, the doctor diagnosed me with Bipolar II.

While at the hospital, I stood before a judge and a few other doctors deciding whether to go home. I had a lawyer and was on trial for trying to kill myself. Talk about trauma on top of trauma. I will never understand persecuting mental health concerns. That was when I finally woke up and wanted to improve my life.

Becoming Amanda Fino

After the psychiatric hospital, I went back home. Dad had a long talk with me. We had a good heart-to-heart, and I was open with him for the first time as we talked about everything under the sun. My dad helped me embrace my cerebral palsy.

He sat me down to explain what my cerebral palsy was. Before, I did not plan to stay with the Finos for too long or love them as I do today; however, they are my soul parents.

How did I become a cerebral palsy self-advocate? It started as me trying to tell Alla I could be one. I opened my Facebook page as "Cerebral Palsy Queen" in November 2015. Yet Back then, I wasn't ready to step forward and become a cerebral palsy self-advocate, unlike I am today. I renamed my cerebral palsy advocate page 'Cerebral Palsy Gal' in 2018. Being late to the game, it was pure luck that no one had taken the name Cerebral Palsy Gal. I wanted to have that name so people would take me seriously. I want to be seen as equal to all, and I am trying my best to educate myself and others about cerebral palsy.

My dear friend Charisse Hogan is a public speaker, artist, YouTube person, cerebral palsy, and anti-bullying advocate. I met her in August of 2012 after finding her Facebook page one night, and I was in awe of seeing a girl like her. Charisse very inspired me. At the time, I was new to the cerebral palsy community of Facebook. Taking a chance, I sent Charisse a private message.

At the time, I did not realize that I even had cerebral palsy. Charisse replied to my message, and since then, I've discovered that cerebral palsy not only affects my walking and talking like my birth mother, Linda, led me to believe. I wish that my parents hadn't had me locked down for half a decade.

Thanks to Charisse, I realized my cerebral palsy made me who I was. I learned about the two cerebral palsy days in March and September. I was shocked that my mom was all right with me being in the cerebral palsy community, but I celebrated my first-ever cerebral palsy Day in September 2012. I have met many people with cerebral palsy since 2012, good and evil, and I am sorry. Guys with cerebral palsy are like any other guys — hitting on me, begging for some nude pictures of me, and yes, one guy showed me a photo of his, you know what. A cerebral palsy woman on Facebook told me she wanted to fly to meet me and have you-know-what, and I just blocked her. Other cerebral palsy men and women have blocked me because of an auto-correct error. Oh well, this is part of life.

Charisse and I became good friends over the years. She once did a YouTube video reviewing my new book, "Wildflower." Through her, I met my very best friend, Heaven Ramsey, and
fellow cerebral palsy self-advocators.

Then out of the blue, Linda called me up one day in 2017, right after I got home from my second O.D. Once again, we tried fixing our relationship. Not even a year had passed before I started stressing about dealing with Linda's mind games again.

In March 2018, she sold F.A.B., the family business, without telling me. I heard the news from a lady who was working there. It took two days for my mom to tell me the story of selling F.A.B. She and Britney had moved somewhere, and she did not even say where she was living because she didn't want the Anderson family or me. I thought she would surprise me on my birthday because she wasn't working.

Whenever I talked to her, she was so happy to talk to me, or she was nasty and made me feel terrible. Britney stopped talking to me because I refused to give her my Fino Netflix password.

On Mother's Day in 2018, Linda told me that Britney got her chocolate-covered strawberries, but I only called her. She hung up on me without telling me that she loved or missed me and wished I had been there. I cried almost all of Mother's Day. She made me so mad that I took it out on my beloved dad and Alla. I was so depressed over her and so fed up with her that I told Linda and Britney goodbye for good. They are a part of my past, and I've filed Linda and Britney away as a memory. Afterward, I felt like life was incredible!

Living in Williamsburg, VA changed my outlook on life and my faith in God. After I let Linda and Britney go, I got back into my beloved writing. My passion finally returned!

What a grand Year 2019!

During that time, I was finishing up writing my first draft of "Cerebral Palsy Gal: A Novella." It was hard. I had two test readers, both of whom had cerebral palsy and were writers. Each of them read it and ripped "cerebral palsy Gal" apart.

One told me: "You make sweeping generalizations about cerebral palsy, and I think a lot of what you say isn't accurate. I've gone through enough of it to get a sense of things, and I don't think this project is anywhere near being ready to be published." She continued to trash my soul.

My other test reader. I sent my new book about living with cerebral palsy to this cerebral palsy woman named Kate. She wanted to assess the read before it came out. Meanwhile, she invited me to join her group for people with disabilities to give hope to one another and empower each other. It turns out that she had read it and hated it. I will not say why. I got out of Katie's Facebook group after I asked her a question. Then one of her friends called me on Facebook, saying bad things about me. I needed clarification about my book. I was on the verge of giving up after getting negative reviews. Then I met Tylia, who was delightful, through my Facebook page. She was a self-advocate for disability, and an author herself Tylia and I became great friends. She read my newly-started "Official Newsletter of the Author Amanda Fino: Cerebral palsy Gal Reader's Nest ." It comes out on the 1st of each month and contains book news, a look at other authors' works, and a 'Badge of Courage' section where it salutes cerebral palsy and other disability warriors. Cerebral palsy Gal Reader's Nest has been my pride and joy since coming out. Tylia sent me a Facebook message asking to be in the following 'Badge of Courage' article. I gave her a copy of the first version of "cerebral palsy Gal."

Tylia loved it. And that is how our friendship blossomed.

Now back to Kelly. She had read my first book, "Omerta Affair," and loved it as it was. She offered a lunch meeting and a contract signing. Wow, I did it! We met up at the restaurant, Food for Thought. My dad went with me, and we hit it off great. In the end, we made a book deal finally! August 17, 2019, titled "Omerta: Timeless Endings." Next, she would read the first version of "cerebral palsy Gal ." If only I knew what I know now, I would have taken a better road. Yet I felt lonely after all the events went down with Ashley and the whole A.D.F. I had nightmares of Ashley and the rest of the group. I lost my friendship with head leader Mary, whom I grew fond of and called my "Virginia Grandma." That hurt me the most. Yet life has once again amazed me.

* * *

I wrote:

I was looking at my Facebook news feed, and I saw that the A.D.F. of Greater Williamsburg had shared your post about The Virginia Board of People with Disabilities (VBPD), which is currently seeking talented, motivated. Resolute advocates to join the 2019-2020 Partners in Policymaking. When the A.D.F. of Greater Williamsburg shared that post, they said: "Do we have any clients interested in this opportunity?" After I read it, I got this unbelievable feeling in my heart and soul, like it was a calling from God. I felt like I needed to be a part of this, to make a difference in the world and speak on behalf of disabled people who can't.

Thank you for considering me as an applicant. I am honored by this fantastic opportunity.

Sincerely, Amanda Forrie

My answer to one of the many questions on their application form was. I took it like I was applying for college. It was due on March 15, 2019. I worked hard, giving all, I had into this application. I worked on it all day on New Year's Day of 2019.

I received my three letters of recommendation. Two of my three letters were written by my dad's friend, Dan Moldea, author of "The Hoffa Wars," and his other friend, James Grady, the author of "Six Days of the Condor." On January 18, I turned it in, proud of myself. I just sat back and waited. Well, this led me to finish authoring this book. It had been a work in progress for years, and I had not found the exact words until then.

May came without a word for the Virginia Board for People with Disabilities. I felt I must have done something wrong that made them reject me. Then on May 7, 2019, I received an email wondering why I still needed to reply to my congratulations letter that they had mailed me in April and whether I still wanted in. I told them, 'Yes'! I still wanted to be a part of Partners in Policymaking. My letter must have gotten lost in the mail. I was shocked to hear that I got in. I had never achieved something this incredible before in my whole lifetime. I did two weeks' worth of work in two days to keep my spot. I loved doing it! It shows what one can do when one puts their heart into something.

One night before my 29th birthday, Ron and Alla asked me if they could adopt me as their daughter, making me Amanda Fino, a real by-law. I told them yes, and Ron and Alla had also gotten my grandma and Papa's blessing.

* * *

Words cannot express my feelings about having a new, loving family and becoming a real daughter that is loved!

In June, I went on the best vacation of my life! Niagara Falls was breathtakingly magnificent. I saw all of Buffalo and New York and ate the best food you can eat there. We went to the art museum and the history museum and the zoo. I saw my first gorilla, and it was just priceless to me. One day we went to the beach on Lake Erie. It was remarkable, to say the least, and filled with beautiful memories.

All summer long, I had to prepare for the first policymaking sessions that would start on Friday, September 13. I had to write out the first 3-minute speech that I would give in Richmond, Virginia, on Saturday, November 2, 2019, during Capitol Day, with a mock testimony panel and as a member of the Virginia Board for People with Disabilities. Writing out a list of issues &

Concerns might require grassroots advocacy to help improve life for everyone with disabilities in my state of Virginia. I also included a few facts about the disability rights movement. I had to admit that I had little/limited knowledge about the history of people with disabilities. Over the summer, I gained experience in this subject. I was requested to read this vast internet textbook, Parallels in Time (A History of Disabilities). I enjoyed it and was impressed by how well I put it together!

Partners in Policymaking: Life-changing

September 13 came fast. I was set to become a participant in the Partners in Policymaking Program (P.I.P.) for the Virginia Board for People with Disabilities. Yet, I was so worried about my temper ruining this new change that God had given me. My parents were worried about me as it was my first time staying a night in a hotel. Especially my mom, who was in Russia worrying to death about me while she was visiting her, well, my new side of my family.

Was it a test? If so, I passed it with excellence! I had no blow-ups while studying hard at a five-star hotel in Newport News, V.A., along with other people with disabilities and parents with disabled kids.

It was a unique group of all kinds of people that was led by three outstanding ladies: Nena, Jettie, and Dr. Pamela, who is now my mentor.

We were feeling blessed, thankful, and thrilled to participate in this. It was extraordinary how much it impacted my life in the short time since we met. I've found that meeting a new group of people was much better than being the 'new girl.' I gave my first speech on November 2, 2019, in the heart of Richmond. It was a remarkable day that I hold close to my heart.

I spent two days lobbying in the heart of Richmond, Virginia, telling my delegates and state senators that we needed to find a cure for cerebral palsy.

It was an incredible experience. It was a high honor to be sitting in the senate gallery. Sometimes, I am blown away by what God has planned for me... ¦ What I wrote for my last P.I.P. project will do justice in explaining my time in P.I.

***

To my fantastic P.I.P. teachers and classmates, I want to thank you all for these life-changing experiences that each of you has given me since September 13, 2019. It's a day that I shall hold dear to my heart. Thanks to all of you, I feel like I'm blossoming before your eyes! I have done things that I have never done before.

When I got my homework assignment, I asked one of my friends for all the 411 on our legislators since she was in the know. My dad knew our senator from working with him in the courts since my dad is a P.I. my rounds of emails to each of them were sent on September 20, 2019, around eight A.M. Almost two months went by, and I am still waiting for a reply. I didn't want to email them again, and I had no one to help me call each of them. I had no idea what to do, and I worried about it. I emailed Dr. Pamela and told her that I felt like I was failing the class. Dr. Pamela replied to me, telling me not to panic. Jettie would help me. Jettie helped via email as I set up a meeting with the senator's legislative aide on November 10 at nine A.M. at my senator's office in my town, Williamsburg.

I thought that I was ready to rock and roll. I brought my dad with me, and we would knock it out of the park together! Yet, I discovered that I needed to prepare for this meeting. I was on time; parking was secure. Not all life experiences are positive. I met with his aid and an intern, whose name I still need to get. It was all lip service. To me, they met with me just because I was a voter. His aid informed me that there is a 95% chance that the state will pass the legalization of medical marijuana in Virginia. Even the state would support the legalization of marijuana, as I told him what the legalization of medical marijuana could do in the state for people with cerebral palsy. Once the meeting finished, I felt like crap. My speech did not have an impact on him at all. The only thing I did right was get a photo with the aid. I posted it on Facebook with a tag of my senator, but they then took the tag off of the picture. The next day I wrote him a thank-you email, and I didn't get any reply. Now, I'm taking steps to ensure that does not happen in the future.

My Grand Day of Advocacy in Richmond!

I have got to love how life works in mysterious ways. I was at an author's dinner in the heart of Washington, DC, when I got an email from Dr. Pamela inviting us to a town hall meeting with a delegate. I replied right back, telling Dr. Pamela that I wanted to go — thinking this was my chance to make up for my mistake with my senator. Then Christine, one of my classmates and a new friend, invited everyone in P.I.P. to the State Special Education Advisory Committee (S.S.E.A.C.). The beginning start of my grand day of advocacy in Richmond, thanks to some fantastic people. That day was another avenue I explored to engage with my legislators, including meeting with the Delegates. I observed the S.S.E.A.C. meeting the whole day, taking notes and staying quiet. I re-gave my P.I.P. testimony from Capitol Day when it was time for public comments. I was starting 2020 off with a bang as a change agent for Virginians with disabilities with Alexis at Virginia Public Budget Hearings. It was an experience all by itself.

I looked forward to D.D. Day (Developmental Disabilities Day), February 6, 2020! In class, we had discussed what bills were up on the block for this year's D.D. Day. Family Life Education/Healthy Relationships had a mirroring bill in the Senate that stood out to me. I once more tried to email my new Delegate and senator.

Hours later, I jumped with pure joy. I had a 9 A.M. meeting with my Delegate's legislative aide. I was notified that my Delegate would join us if her schedule permitted. I did this all on my own, with no help. That was a big step since this was the first time I had made an appointment. I started getting prepared for this up-and-coming D.D. day with my short speech. It never hurts when you have your P.I.P. classmates behind you that I shall take to the meeting. "We are the people!"

The P.I.P. legislative meeting experience was t of trial and error that gave me my first grand adventure.

I am very blessed by God to come out of this as a more robust and better human being. I am considering writing a fictional book about my P.I.P. experience. It is a part of life. Live and learn. I wish that I could write all about my D.D. Day. I am happy yet sad that P.I.P. is over because I will miss each of them. We did it! We are the class of 2020!

* * *

Due to COVID-19, we missed our huge graduation ceremony, which was to be on April 4, 2020.

Good evening, my brothers and sisters. I can't believe that tonight is our baccalaureate service. I am glad to be standing here a P.I.P. While I reflect on these past six months and 21 days, I realize that I only have two minutes. How on earth do I express how much P.I.P. has meant to me? I was thinking about what to say in my hotel room the morning after I received the paper while listening to music. The song "Hotel California" started to play. It hit me that this song fits my P.I.P. reflections. We met in a hotel to learn, share a lot, and form unbreakable bonds. It makes me believe this is mine, "Hotel Virginia!" I found my voice with you while telling all of you some of my deep, dark secrets. I did so many incredible things, many of them for the first time, as I tested myself and passed. Along the way, I found my true passion for being a disability self-advocate. I want to change the way the world thinks about people with disabilities. The love that each of you showed me still astonishes me. I am finding myself becoming a better person. Cheers to us, The P.I.P. class of 2020, with best wishes for what comes next in your life path! Always remember this: "We are the people!"

In December 2019, I released the book Cerebral Palsy Gal: A Novella, which has been in production for many years. I'm curious where I got the strength to write cerebral palsy Gal after asking for it many times. Although I was very proud of this accomplishment, I was very hurt when one girl damaged my autobiography and my name a day after it was released. In my opinion, I am partly responsible for causing Cerebral Palsy Gal: A Novella" to be placed on my publisher blacklist, making it unpublished after a few months.

I cut ties with the publisher. After I revised the book, I called it Living Strong with Cerebral Palsy, which appeared in March of 2021. I had to hide an editor who tried to sabotage me and my book by making grammatical errors or other mistakes to sabotage it. I retitled the piece Eternal Sunshine of a cerebral palsy Gal's Mind thanks to my friend, who helped me fix it. My decision to take the book off the shelf was due to personal reasons.

It had been so painful for me. People have contacted me via Facebook and trashed my book in the past. I have tried to help people, but they all end up hurting me. As it turns out, this is what often happens in the cerebral palsy community quite often. Everyone is in it for themselves and doesn't want to help anyone else. As a result, everyone is constantly competing with one another, trying to beat one another and outdo one another. It was tough on me until I met my friend, Jesus.

One day I was chatting to Heaven, my friend, about having some issues with people with cerebral palsy and why it's sometimes hard. Heaven just told me this: some of the "cerebral palsy" self-advocates on the Facebook community viewed it like an ongoing beauty pageant. She was right. All the missing parts I had seen on Facebook over the years fit together.

2020: May I Say Any More

I have not openly chatted about what effects this year, Covid-19, and the Black Lives Matter movement have had on my life and thoughts. Yet, it is time. In March, I felt like a rock star. I was at the top of the world, passing my P.I.P. class, graduating, and turning 30 years old simultaneously. Then March 13, 2020, happened. It was just as bad as September 11, 2001. That Friday was indeed my Friday, the 13th. My graduation ceremony was temporarily canceled because of covid, and I was informed that it would be later. Seven people had Covid-19 in my county. Since Friday the 13th, my life has changed forever.

Not soon after that, my dad tested positive for the Coronavirus. It was unbearable for my soul to stay far away from a loved one. Thanks to the great Lord, dad beat Covid-19.

For the U.S. When Covid-19 struck, the U.S.A. went into lockdown for 55 days. The Covid-19 pandemic has not been fun for me or; my anger and sadness. During the lockdown, I was stressing out., worrying, and losing sleep. I cried for the lives we lost and the ones we are still losing.

Two simple, heartfelt words came into my mind just now. "I care." I care about all humans. We are all equal, and our blood is the same color. Only a few people positively expressed my point of view.

On May 25, the killing of George Floyd made me sad. The violent protests horrified me, and this continued over the summer. All I can say about this matter is that two wrongs don't make a right.

Since the shutdown, people with disabilities have stayed at home and couldn't go out. As a nation, we have developed ways to stay together at home while staying safe. In these new ways of life, Zoom, YouTube, and other platforms have made it easier for people with disabilities to fit in. The Access program allows them to participate in church activities, book signings, community events, town hall meetings, etc. Before Covid-19, we could not do these things because of our disabilities.

I now understand why my friend would say that year was like a 'Disability Revolution.' I can feel that a new disability movement is happening while I am writing this. July was the 30 anniversary of the A.D.A., and I was busy being a cerebral palsy advocate. I was getting all set for the A.D.A. 30TH ANNIVERSARY, Virginia style. I was grateful to be a part of this whole jam-packed week. It all led up to the DAY OF ACTION, SATURDAY, J.U.L.Y. 25TH, when I had to deliver a small part of a tremendous speech. I had become a board member of the Partnership's Constabulary Board because of pure luck.

* * *

In August 2020, my Grand Papa Joseph turned 91, and I wish to say it was a happy event. On the morning of his birthday, he was so weak that grandma had to call 911. On September 18, 2020, he joined God in Heaven.

I didn't fly out to say my farewells to my Grand Papa. I was planning on going, though, because I'd never gotten to say goodbye to my grandma Forrie. In the end, it was Covid-19 that interfered with my travel plans. I called my Papa one last time while he still remembered who I was. Grand Papa was upbeat, so glad, and thankful to get me out of the hole they had made me in the shop. It was a better-sweet phone convention.

We had a service for him, just a small one. Thanks to Uncle Chuck and Aunt Lily, it was virtual. I felt blessed to be at my beloved grandfather's funeral services. Uncle Chuck, Aunt Lily, Uncle David, Aunt Shelby, James, Alyssa, Alex, and I took turns holding the phone up, so I felt like I was in person.

Life would never be the same, yet our family has a new guardian angel. A month before September 18, my Uncle Frank Cullotta lost his fight with Covid-19 and passed on. It took me by surprise when my dad told me he had died while bringing in our morning coffee.

Ron had gotten the call after I had gone to bed. He almost woke me up to tell me because he did not want me to find out via social media before I did not check my phone like I always did when I first woke up. That morning, the morning coffee was in honor of Uncle Frank Cullotta.

That fall, Alla and I started to go on walks, walking through our neighborhood and onto the wood walking trail. It has helped me with my moods and so much more health-wise. I loved walking with my new mom Alla.

Godmother and I

It is only a minor complaint on my part that I decided not to include someone very close to me, my Godmother since I didn't have any idea of what had happened to her, but I do think it would be an excellent ending for the tale that I have written.

Las Vegas in 1989, Two women, Liz and Linda, were eating lunch at Taco Bell, talking about Linda and her husband of nine years. They have tried hard to create a baby using a regular method for years. The couple had given up hopes of a baby and used their savings to build a pool. Linda complained to Liz about feeling a bit queasy and didn't know why. As Liz asked when Linda's last period was, Linda was prompted to believe that her period was late.

After finishing their lunch, the two rushed to a nearby drugstore. It was Liz who had purchased a Clearblue Easy Pregnancy Test for Linda, thinking that Linda may be pregnant, yet Linda was in disbelief. At that point, Linda used the pharmacy bathroom to see whether she was, in fact, pregnant.

They waited for three minutes, and the test showed yes, Linda was expecting a child.

Still, Linda could not believe it.

They purchased all kinds of pregnancy tests to ensure that Linda was expecting a child.

When the results of all tests were positive, Linda named Liz the Godmother of her newly discovered child within her. This baby in Linda's tummy was me!

While growing up, Liz was a big part of my life, and Liz was like a second mother.

I called her my Godmommy despite never being baptized in the Christian faith; it always keeps me in awe, even to this day.

Neither side of my family was a church-going Christian family. Godmommy gifted me things from the Bible and VHSs from a Christian perspective during my childhood. I recall a video of someone saying, "Jesus says Let the children come to me." When I was three years old, my godmom married someone that I came called my Uncle.

Even though she celebrated her birthday the day after mine, my Godmother was always at my birthdays.

She never missed any significant life marks in my childhood until my family moved away from Las Vegas when I was seven.

I remember a cold winter day, holding my baby godbrother when he came home from the hospitalhelping her first daughter. I remember her taking me to Burger King and getting my first crown.

I was about eleven, and my Godfamliy packed up their family home and sold it.

They wanted to be closer to their family back east while raising their child, who was very far away, in a different time zone. To me, as a kid, it was a sad day indeed.

The last time I saw my Godmom was when I was 14. They visited a friend's house, so I enjoyed the short period. Godmom asked me to fly back for a month, but 9/11 was still fresh in my head. I used to feel bad about not going, but it was not in God's plans.

It felt like I was about to turn 18 when Linda and Liz both got so busy that they stopped communicating regularly.

Three days after my 32nd birthday, a message from Liz appeared on my Facebook timeline when I woke up. I was shocked and happy, reading her message over and over. Then replying, I've never stopped loving her.

In June 2021, I was blessed to visit my Godmother, Uncle, and family. When I first saw my godmom at the airport, the overwhelming feeling of my love and seeing her was remarkable, like I'd found a missing part of my heart I'd been looking for all my life.

I enjoyed every moment of my trip being back with family, being with my little godbrothers and godsister. My godbrother, whom I held as a newborn, grew even taller. I even went to church with them, so I started thinking about finding my church.

Since then, Godmom and I have communicated daily. It is beautiful to renew the relationship we lost many years ago like it was how the Lord wanted it to be.

We went to the beach this past year, just us two for our birthdays. This trip will always be a jewel in my memory!

Cabin 8 in Mammoth Mountain

THIS IS A REAL GHOST STORY!
Note: I wanted to share this, but it did not fit in the central part of the book.
The 4th of July in 2006 was coming up, and my dad wanted to go fishing and stay in a cabin on Mammoth Mountain, California, for the weekend. It was a last-minute decision, so I was helping my mom find a cabin to rent. The mountain cabins were sold out for the fourth until a woman called my mom back, telling her that while all the cabins were sold out, cabin eight was available, but it was a two-story cabin. The lady told my mom that she would give it to us as long as we did not use the upper part of the cabin. That was fine with my mom because it would only be my parents, my little sister, Britney, and me. I remember my mom saying, "How about cabin number 8, Amanda?" An odd feeling came over me. I was not too fond of the number eight. I tried to voice my opinion, but it was the last cabin on that mountain. We took it because dad needed to get away from work and relax with a fishing pole in the lake.
'On July 1, 2006, we drove up to where the cabin's rental office was. We ended up getting lost, and my parents were looking for directions. A dog didn't take his eyes off me the whole time we were in the office. I looked right into the dog's eyes, and I felt like the dog was looking at my soul. I felt an odd connection between this dog and me. Bizarre, right?

When my family got to the right cabin rental office, they told us that they were still cleaning the cabin and it would be more than an hour until they finished. It was fishy because it was past check-in time. We went to a small store nearby that we passed on our way in, bought our fishing license and some food, returned to the office, and waited for the key.

We got the key to cabin 8, and all went up. We were so excited to spend the weekend relaxing and having family time. When we opened the front door, there was a weird little door in front of the stairs, and my dad tried to open it; The cabin was locked from within. So, we said, "Oh well!" and continued to unpack the car. There were two rooms downstairs.

My parents took one, and Britney and I took the other, which had a full bed and a twin. I took the twin bed because I love twin beds. After we unpacked, I had to use the bathroom. When I used the bathroom, I felt so weird after I looked at the shower. There was a tiny hole in the wall. I was so scared and decided that there was no way I would take a shower there. I shook it off and went to the kitchen table, and the whole family played cards until dinner. That night we had a ready-made Hamburger Helper and watched Kate Hudson in The Skeleton Key. When it was bedtime, we all went to bed simultaneously. That is when things began. I heard weird noises and footsteps. First, it was upstairs. Soon, it was closer. Not only were their strange noises, but I also had a terrible feeling. I faced the wall and looked at it since I was so scared. Soon my mom ran into the room, causing me to turn in bed to look at her. She said nothing and got in the same bed as Britney. I turned back to the wall and looked at it until I fell asleep.

I woke up at the same time as my mom, crawling a bit off the bed, got my Ghostbusters DVD cover, and held it up in the air, showing my mom. She shook her head, letting out a little laugh, and smiled at me while she gave me a thumbs up.

That morning was very odd. We only really talked once when my mom told us that a drive would be good for us. Once we got out of cabin eight, I realized there was no sign of wildlife, and I had never heard a bird sing or seen chipmunks or squirrels on the deck or around that cabin.

Once in the car, my mom told us that someone was playing with her hair while in bed with my dad, and that is why she ran in and jumped in bed with Britney. Mom also asked all of us who was the one who kept closing the bathroom window because she had it open and always found it shut. No one in the car said they had shut that window.

We then saw a big, new 5-star resort, The Village Lodge, in Mammoth. My parents decided to see if the resort had any available rooms because the whole family was freaked out about returning to cabin 8. Luckily, they had a two-bedroom condo available, and my parents took it and didn't care about the cost. My dad told my mom and me to stay at the resort and relax while he and Britney returned to cabin 8 to get all our belongings.

They told us that they would be right back, an hour top. We just relaxed there with no worries. A long time passed, and they were still waiting for word from them. Inside the resort was a small shopping center. My mom and I walked window-shopping around it to pass the time. We hoped that dad and Britney would be in the condominium when we returned. When we got back, they were not there. My mom called dad's and Britney's cell phones. Now we were so worried and did not know what to do. I felt sick to my stomach. Happy 4th of July, Amanda, I thought when they finally showed up. My dad and Britney were pale white. They told us that things began happening when they returned to pack up – unexplained things. When my dad was getting his gun down from the closet, he saw it unlocked and pointed at him. My dad had it locked with the gun pointing at the closet wall. They believed something or someone did not want them to leave cabin eight. While they packed, things kept happening that they could not explain. They decided to pack room by room together until they were done.

They left cabin 8 with all of our belongings. They stopped at the main office to return the key and said we couldn't stay because of a family emergency. The owner of cabin eight would have to wait to give my dad a refund on that cabin. My dad did not care and got out of there, freaking out. They missed the highway exit back to the resort and didn't realize it until twenty minutes later because they both were in a state of horror.

All that mattered was cabin 8 was over, and we were safe. My dad didn't even relax on the lake fishing after what happened.

Epilogue

I pray for a cure for cerebral palsy. I am all for stem cell research for cerebral palsy. Until that day, I'm happy with my family and friends. I happily enjoy my blessed life, whether chatting with Heaven or texting my beloved Godmother. Since becoming a born- Christian, I have become an integral part of my church and made new friends. By enabling me to become a better woman and grow in grace and truth.

After joining my church, I experienced the hope and joy I found in God. I continue to have a lot of work on my part through the Spirit to overcome situations like anger, fear, shame, and doubt when they arise in me as they arise within me.

Cyndi was a significant key person who played a big role in my growth in grace. We met in the adult Sunday school hour, then I switched to Monday morning women's bible study, and she happened to be one of the teachers. It is a mystery how God works, but Cyndi's family embraced me as a very close friend, and together we are writing a book as she guides me in the ways of the Christian woman. The amount of gratitude I owe Cyndi is beyond words.

These are just a few things the enemy uses to discourage Christians or make them doubt God's love for them.

Our world is broken, which exposes us to sin, and is filled with pain and heartbreak caused by sinful people. It causes us to feel sad and broken. Oddly enough, I was drawn to my beloved church and its people through this journey.

My life has been filled with events that have left me angry and hurt. The frustration I felt due to my cerebral palsy and speech disorder and feeling so misunderstood also turned into anger. The emotions I was experiencing were beyond my ability to handle until I gave my life to God. As a Christian, I'm still working on letting go of past anger and hurt through the grace of God. He will lead this process, and I am thankful for this new beginning.

Several months ago, I felt like the Holy Spirit had guided me to create a flyer for the church newsletter that explained how to welcome disabled adults into the church. God guided me to finding my true calling, allowing me to share my story of coming to faith with disabled people, telling them about God's love, and exploring ways in which they could fly despite their disabilities.

CP Gal's World is my YouTube channel, where I make videos regularly. CP: Gal's World is a YouTube channel I intend to turn into a mission to serve the world.

I have a passion in my heart to make our churches more inclusive of those with disabilities. I want to educate people on how to accept them. My birth dad Matt Forrie is one of the most influential people in my life, and I miss him more than anything else. I can't go a day without thinking about my dad and how young we were when he joined Jesus and his father, God. My new father, Ron, posted this on his Facebook timeline on December 2022.

"Amanda Forry is now our adopted daughter.- Amanda Forry, who has Cerebral Palsy, has been Officially adopted by my wife and me. Approximately eight years ago, I received a phone call from Nevada Social Services that they found Amanda living on the streets of Las Vegas. Her father died, and her mother and sister no longer wanted her. They found my business card (I met her when I gave a speech in Vegas) in her possessions. Like most, I did not know what to do. I was informed that because she was an adult, there was little they could do. I tried friends and even contacted California. I found Amanda's

Grandmother, Ann, who told me the whole story. After my attempts proved futile, I told the Social Service representative. To put her on a plane, and we will take care of her. It was not all peaches N cream, The screaming and hitting became almost impossible, but we hung in. I learned much more about the cruelty, rape, and suffering this human being went through. Unbelievable, truly unbelievable. Now Amanda is a wonderful young lady and a true blessing to us. She is a published Author (I never helped), and we are very proud of her."

As I said, it was a great blessing knowing I have a real family. I have my coffee with my new dad at home all the time and watch the news together each morning when we walk up walking with My new mom afterward, relaxing in our beautiful backyard and having tea together. I visit my godfamily down in Georgia once a year. Life is such a blessing! As far as dating is concerned, I have tried to date other men, but I have not been able to do so because of Scott. On one of the days, Grragwa called me and said she had spoken with Scott one day and wanted to let me know. After she told him what I had been up to back in Virginia, he was so proud of me that he could hardly contain his excitement. As a result, Scott explained to grandma that he loved me and that I was the one he loved most. The love he has for me will never fade. Although Scott would have loved to marry me, he was too old and

Keep up with me. Something within me refused to date anyone as soon as I heard this.

My mind sometimes goes into a fog, but I can escape it. Each day I want to better myself, and I keep my demons at bay. I never really can forgive Scarlett for what she did. Life might have been better if Scarlett wasn't in it. I might have gone to college if my dad had not died.

I wouldn't trade my new life now for all the tea in China. As John Lennon once said, "Life is what happens when you are busy making other plans."

IN CLOSING

I hope you recognize that my condition still limits the amount I can put on paper filled with grammatical flaws. I am overcoming and moving into writing and reading every day. I love the reality of Jack London's stories, The visually poetic Shakespeare, Kahlil Gibran.Mark Twain, and Boris Pasternak. After reading, I am filled with a desire to learn more. A relentless haunt to put my thoughts and dreams on paper. I am filled with the dream of being the author, understanding my limitations caused by my having cerebral palsy, yet moving into a realm of can-do. I really want to prove that having a disability can be overcome and a focal point for those that feel for us yet cannot understandably fathom that we, too, have the very same feelings as yours. We are trying to be recognized by all that we are a group of people through no fault of our own have limitations.

It is tough not being able to do the things we want to. As you just read, I have had a difficult time between suffering abuse and love from those that genuinely care. It's not a pity that we desire but no strings attached friendship and love. "That's all." I do want to continue the quest to write and then write some more. My desire is to write stories for children and those suffering from mental and physical conditions. From the bottom of my heart, I thank you all for understanding.

God Bless

[ ]